Alfred Todd

A treatise on the proceedings to be adopted in conducting or

opposing private bills in the Parliament of Canada

Alfred Todd

A treatise on the proceedings to be adopted in conducting or opposing private bills in the Parliament of Canada

ISBN/EAN: 9783337152642

Printed in Europe, USA, Canada, Australia, Japan

Cover: Foto ©Andreas Hilbeck / pixelio.de

More available books at **www.hansebooks.com**

A TREATISE

ON THE

PROCEEDINGS TO BE ADOPTED

IN CONDUCTING OR OPPOSING

PRIVATE BILLS

IN THE

Parliament of Canada;

AND THE

STANDING ORDERS OF BOTH HOUSES

IN RELATION THERETO.

BY ALFRED TODD,
CHIEF CLERK OF COMMITTEES AND PRIVATE BILLS,
HOUSE OF COMMONS.

THIRD EDITION,
EMBRACING THE LATEST CHANGES IN THE PRACTICE.

—

OTTAWA:
PUBLISHED BY JOHN DURIE & SON, SPARKS STREET.
1868.

HUNTER, ROSE & COMPANY, PRINTERS.

PREFACE.

In the first Session of the first Parliament of the Dominion, the Rules and Practice in force in the old Province of Canada with regard to Private Bills were adopted by Parliament, with some modifications in the details, which, though of importance in their place, effected no material alteration in the system. These are all embodied in the present Edition of this work; and as no clearly defined Private Bill system of practice has prevailed in the Local Legislatures of Nova Scotia and New Brunswick, the precedents referred to are all taken from Canadian practice; they include those given in the last Edition, and others gleaned from subsequent legislation, both in the Provincial Parliament, and in the first Session of that of the Dominion.

In the course of the last mentioned Session, it happened upon several occasions, that doubts arose as to the true interpretation of those provisions of the " British North America Act " which placed certain classes of subjects under the exclusive control of the General Parliament, and of the Provincial Legislatures, respectively. A chapter has therefore been added, on " Legislative Jurisdiction," in which mention is made of the various questions that arose from time to time, and the course taken thereon ; and certain observa-

tions and suggestions are offered, in the hope that some plan may
be devised for obtaining a more definite interpretation of the
Imperial Act in this respect.

The authorities cited in explanation of the Imperial practice,
are :—

Report on the practice of the House of Commons upon Private
Bills : with suggestions for the future regulation of Private Busi-
ness in the Legislative Assembly of Canada.   By ALPHEUS TODD,
Librarian to the Legislative Assembly.   (1847.)

Report from Select Committee of the House of Commons on the
Business of the House.   (1861.)

MAY on the Law, Privileges, Proceedings, and Usage of Parliament.   Sixth edition.   (1868.)

SHERWOOD on the proceedings to be adopted in conducting Private Bills through the House of Commons.   Third edition.   (1834.)

FRERE'S Practice of Committees of the House of Commons, with
reference especially to Private Bills.   (1846.)

BRISTOWE on Private Bill legislation in the Imperial Parliament.   (1859.)

HOUSE OF COMMONS,
        OTTAWA, November, 1868.

PREFACE TO THE FIRST EDITION.

THE object of this work, is to explain fully the proceedings at the various stages, in either House, and in Committee, upon Private Bills solicited in the Parliament of Canada. The system of practice, though based on that adopted in the Imperial Parliament, differs from it materially in many of the details; and the absence of any hand-book or guide to the course of proceedings to be observed, has been long felt, not only by parties soliciting or opposing Bills, but also by Members of the Legislature charged with the conduct of such Bills in either House.

The writer has been connected with the Private Bill Office since its establishment, and has thus had an opportunity of noting down, as they occurred, the various decisions and modifications which have been made from time to time, and which have established the system of practice as it now stands; while in all matters not specially provided for, reference is made (in accordance with a Standing Order) to the usages of the Imperial Parliament.

The Rules of the two Houses concerning Private Bills are appended to the work. The Provincial precedents referred to (based on decisions or practice, in the House or in Committee,) will be found in the Journals of the Legislative Assembly (the present system having been but recently introduced into the Upper House).

LEGISLATIVE ASSEMBLY,
    QUEBEC, May, 1862.

PREFACE TO THE SECOND EDITION.

THE first edition of this Treatise was published early in the Session of 1862, when the new Rules adopted by the Legislative Council assimilating the practice of the two Houses first came into operation. Certain modifications of the Rules and practice, calculated to define more clearly the requirements of the Rules, and the powers of the Committee on Standing Orders, and also to facilitate the transaction of business between the two Houses, were suggested in the course of the Session, and these having been agreed upon by the Private Bill Committee of each House, were embodied in Reports to the Legislative Council and Legislative Assembly, respectively, and received their concurrence.

The alterations thus made, though comparatively unimportant, rendered it desirable that a new edition of this work should be issued; and the Committee of the Legislative Assembly having specially recommended that this should be done, a second edition has been prepared accordingly, embodying the changes above referred to, and also the precedents established by decisions and practice in the year 1862.

LEGISLATIVE ASSEMBLY,

QUEBEC, July, 1862.

CONTENTS.

APPENDIX.

PROCEEDINGS

TO BE ADOPTED IN CONDUCTING

PRIVATE BILLS

THROUGH THE

PARLIAMENT OF CANADA.

1.—PRELIMINARY OBSERVATIONS.

The distinction between Public and Private Bills is one that has been recognized and acted upon by the Parliament of the Mother Country from a very early period, and the mode of proceeding upon the two classes of bills has also differed in some important particulars. In passing Private Bills, while Parliament still exercises its legislative functions, its proceedings ~~also~~ partake also of a judicial character; the parties interested in such bills appear as suitors, while those who apprehend injury are admitted as adverse parties to the suit.

Much of the formality of a Court of Justice is

Distinction between Public and Private Bills.

maintained; conditions are required to be observed and their observance proved by the promoters of a bill, and if they abandon it and no other parties take it up, the bill is dropped, however sensible the House may be of its value.*

First provision for Private Bills in Canada

Although this distinction was recognized by the Legislature of the old "Province of Canada" in framing Rules for its guidance at its first Session (in 1841) by the adoption of a provision requiring two months' notice of applications for private bills, and the exaction of a fee of £20 on all such bills ; and also by the appointment, every Session, of a Standing Committee on Private Bills; little else was done towards the adoption of a regular system of practice until the year 1846, when the Speaker of the Legislative Assembly was authorized to cause an inquiry to be made into the system pursued in the House of Commons, with a view to the preparation of a system of Standing Orders and practice adapted to the circumstances of the Province.† The result of this was laid on the table of the House in the following Session,

Alpheus Todd's Report on Private Bill Practice.

in the shape of a Report, prepared by Mr. Alpheus Todd, the present Librarian of the Canadian House of Commons, giving a full and lucid explanation of the system of practice in operation

---

* May, p. 633.

† Assembly Journ., 1846, p. 344.

in the Imperial Parliament, and submitting a code
of orders and regulations such as appeared suit-
able to the requirements of Canada.* No immediate action was taken upon this Report, but
in the same Session the practice of referring both
petitions and bills to the Committee on Private
Bills indiscriminately was discontinued, and
petitions were from that time referred to the
Committee on Standing Orders, for proof of a
compliance with the Rules of the House. In Private
Bill Office.
1850, a Private Bill Office was established, in pursuance of a suggestion contained in the above-
mentioned Report, and a system of practice
organised, which, with some few modifications
subsequently in the details, is that now in use.

Up to the year 1861, no regulations had been Former
practice in
made by the Legislative Council of Canada con- L. Council.
cerning private bills, except to require an official
report to the Speaker of the notices given on
petitions, and the payment of a fee on all such
bills as originated in that House: but in the Session of 1861, a conference was held between the
two Houses, which led to the adoption, by the
Council, of the Private Bill Rules of the Assembly *verbatim et literatim.*† These Rules were
slightly modified in succeeding Sessions, and, in

* Assembly Journ., 1847, p. 31. (App. B.)
† L. Council Journ., 1861, pp. 98, 104.

the first Session of the Parliament of Canada held
Practice in both Houses now nearly identical. under the authority of the "British North America Act, 1867," they were adopted by both Houses, with some further modifications as regards the Commons, which were not made in the Rules of the Senate; the Rules as adopted by each House, will be found at the end of this work, (Appendix I,) together with certain additional Rules of the Senate relating to Divorce Bills. (Appendix II.)

The practice of the two Houses being thus made almost identical, the account given in the following pages, of the proceedings on Petitions and Bills in the Lower House, will apply substantially to the Upper, any diversity of practice between the two Houses being specially pointed out in the appropriate place. It should be stated, however, that the fee is charged only in the House in which the bill originates,* and all expenses for printing and translation being exacted at the same time, no payment is required to be made in the other House, except in cases where a bill is ordered to be reprinted, when the expense must be borne **In which House Private Bills may originate.** by its promoters. As a general rule, private bills may originate in either House, but it being the exclusive right of the Commons to impose and appropriate all charges imposed upon the people, every bill which involves any tax, rate, toll, or

---

* 58th Rule.

duty, ought to be first brought into that House.* It has followed from this restriction that by far the greater number of private bills have been first passed by the Lower House.† It may be worthy of consideration whether it might not be desirable, in this country, also to include bills relating to Banking in this category, as they are necessarily subject to the supervision of the Minister of Finance, who has always a seat in the Commons. The Lords have generally originated naturalization, name, estate, and divorce bills,‡ but this has not been the practice with the Upper House, in this country, save only as regards divorce bills, which have invariably been introduced first into that House.

The House of Commons of Great Britain, by a Standing Order of 1858 (No. 67), have provided that the Chairman of Ways and Means, shall, at the commencement of each Session, confer with the Chairman of Committees of the House of Lords, for the purpose of determining in which

Arrangement between the two Houses for originating bills.

---

* May. pp. 437, 635.

† The House of Commons of Great Britain, by a Standing Order of 27th July, 1858, have agreed " that this House will not insist on its privileges with regard to any clauses in private bills sent down from the House of Lords, which refer to tolls and charges for services performed, and are not in the nature of a tax."

‡ May, p. 636.

House the respective private bills should be first
considered, and report the same to the House.*
This arrangement was the result of a recommen-
dation contained in the 3rd Report of the Select
Committee of the House of Commons on Private
Bills, in 1847. (p. 6.)

* Bristowe's Private Bill Practice, pp. 15, 73. An example
of the result of this arrangement will be seen by referring to the
Commons Journals of 1860, p. 16.

2.—DEFINITION OF A PRIVATE BILL.

Every bill for the particular interest or benefit of any person or persons, is treated as a private bill, whether it be for the interest of an individual, a public company or corporation, a parish, a city, a county, or other locality; * it is equally distinguished from a measure of public policy in which the whole community are interested, and this distinction is marked by the solicitation of private bills by the parties whose interests are concerned.† *(margin: Distinction between Public and Private Bills.)*

There is a class of bills, however, which, though local or special in their operation, yet having been solicited by persons not in the interest of the parties to be affected by their operation, or having been introduced upon public grounds, have been treated by the Legislature as public bills. Bills of this class have occasionally been introduced as private, and referred to the Standing Committee *(margin: Semi-private bills.)*

---

* A bill for the benefit of three Counties has been held by the British House of Commons to be a private bill. 1 Commons Journ., p. 393.

† May, p. 626.

on Private Bills, but upon their report that they
were public, rather than private in their character, they have been referred by the House to another committee, and treated otherwise as public
bills.* It must be obvious, however, that on bills
of this nature, the same notice should be required
as upon a private bill, with the exception only of
such as are introduced upon some well-defined
principle of public policy or right.

Victoria
New Town-
ships Bill.
(L. Assem-
bly.) In 1858, the Committee on Private Bills reported, with reference to a bill to attach certain newly
surveyed townships to the County of Victoria,
that they were in doubt whether the bill came
within their province, inasmuch as it affected the
Territorial Divisions of the Province, the Representation, and the administration of Justice ; but
they prepared such amendments as appeared to
them desirable, and left it to the House to consider whether action should be taken on their report or not. The House took the bill into consideration with the proposed amendments, and
treated it therefore as a private bill.† In 1864,
the same course was taken (with a like result) in

---

* Quebec Recorder's Court, 1856 : Montreal Trinity House
(amending the provisions concerning pilotage), 1857; Quebec
Harbour (a Government Trust), 1858; River Welland Bridges
Protection, 1859 ; Caisse d'Economie de St. Roch Investigation,
1861; Rimouski and Gaspé division, 1865.

† Assembly Journ., 1858, pp. 568, 631.

reference to a bill respecting the Common of the Huron Indians at Lorette. which was not considered private, the Indians being under the special protection of the Crown.*

Common of Lorette Indians Bill. (do.)

In the British House of Commons, may be instanced the Passing Tolls on Shipping Bill (introduced in 1856). which was held to be a public bill. It concerned the harbours of Dover. Ramsgate, Whitby and Bridlington, abolished passing tolls. transferred the control of those harbours to the Board of Trade, imposed tolls, and repealed local Acts; but, being a measure of general policy, its character was not changed by the fact that these harbours only came under its operation. The Red Sea and India Telegraph Bill (in 1861), which amended a private Act, was introduced and passed as a public bill, as it concerned the conditions of a government guarantee.† The practice in Canada has been to treat all Bills relating to the Representation,‡ the administration of Justice,§ or the protection of the Indians

Passing Tolls on Shipping Bill. (Commons).

Red Sea and India Telegraph Bill. (do.)

---

* Assembly Journ., 1864, pp. 391, 478.

† May, p. 629.

‡ Armagh Representation, 1858; Peel do., 1858; Drummond and Arthabaska do., 1858 ; Bill to transfer Delaware from the West to the East Riding (Electoral Division) of Middlesex, 1862 ; Hochelaga polls, 1863 (Aug. Sess.)

§ Montreal Recorder's Court, 1852-3; Gaspé Circuit Court, 1852-3 ; Huntingdon Circuit Court, 1854-5 ; Montmagny do.,

and their lands and property,* however local or
partial in their operation, as public bills, these
questions being under the especial charge of the
Administration, and being dealt with on broad
general principles. All bills relating to Government Trusts or Commissions,† or public works
under Government control,‡ are likewise so
treated.

Some bills, though strictly private, having
been introduced irregularly (i. e., not based upon
petition. in the usual way), the committee have
declined to proceed upon them.§ In 1864.
a bill to enable the Church Societies and Incorporated Synods of the Church of England Dioceses in Canada to sell the Rectorial lands in the
said Dioceses, having been sent down by the Legislative Council, objection was taken at the second
reading, that the bill was a private one, and
should have been brought in on a petition; and

Sidenotes: Certain bills treated as public bills. Bills introduced irregularly Rectorial lands sale Bill.

1858; Kamouraska Gaol and Court House, 1863 (Aug. Sess.);
Quebec Recorder's Court, 1864 and 1865. See also May, p. 629.

   * Common of Lorette Indians, 1864.

   † Montreal Trinity House, 1857; Quebec Harbour, 1858,
1863, and 1867–8; Montreal Turnpike Road Trust, 1861; Montreal Port Warden, 1862 and 1863 (Feb. Sess.); Montreal Harbour, 1865.

   ‡ Northern Railway, 1859; Intercolonial Railway, 1867–8.
See May, p. 662.

   § Rimouski and Gaspé division, 1865 (Jan. Sess.); Quebec
Corporation, 1866.

the objection being sustained, the bill was not proceeded with.* In 1866, objection was taken, _{Perth Debt Bill.} at the second reading, to a bill to extend the time for paying the debt of the County of Perth (due to the Municipal Loan Fund) that it, though a private bill, affected the public revenue, and should therefore have originated in committee of the whole; and the objection was fatal to the bill.† It has been held that a bill commenced as a private bill cannot be taken up and proceeded with as a public bill.‡

The proceedings observed in the Imperial Par- _{Difference between Imperial and Canadian practice.} liament in the passage of private bills, are neces- sarily somewhat complicated in their character, in consequence of the numerous checks imposed for the protection of the many interests which they may affect or involve; and the expense at- tending these proceedings is considerable : but the different circumstances of this country, as one but newly settled, allowing a freer scope for en- terprise. with comparatively little risk of infring- ing upon existing rights or privileges, admit (for a time at least) of a much simpler and more inex- pensive system of Private Bill legislation. In ex- plaining the system adopted (after various modi-

---

* Assembly Journ., 1865 (Aug. Sess.), p. 123.

† Assembly Journ., 1866, p. 293.

‡ May, p. 631.

Proceedings in Commons to be described first. fications) by our Legislature, it is proposed to state the various forms and proceedings so far as can conveniently be done, in the order in which they occur. from the presentation of the petition (in either House) to the final passage of the bill. It will be convenient for this purpose to begin with the House of Commons, but the course observed in either House being now identical (with the exception of proceedings upon Divorce Bills in the Upper House, which are described in the latter part of this work, and certain matters of detail with reference to private bills generally, which are noticed in the proper place), the description will apply equally to bills originating in the Senate.

3.—LEGISLATIVE JURISDICTION

REGARDING PRIVATE BILLS.

By the provisions of " The British North
America Act, 1867," certain classes of Private
Bills are placed under the exclusive control of
the Parliament of the Dominion, and certain
others are transferred to the Provincial Legislatures.

The classes of subjects which, under this
arrangement, pertain exclusively to the *Parliament of the Dominion*, are thus defined by the Act :

Sec. 91.—Ferries between a Province and any
    British or Foreign Country, or between
    two Provinces.

Banking, Incorporation of Banks, and the issue
    of Paper Money.

Savings Banks.

Patents of Invention and Discovery.

Naturalization and Aliens.

Marriage and Divorce,—and

Such classes of subjects as are expressly excepted

2

Subjects under control of Parliament.

in the enumeration of the classes of subjects by this Act assigned exclusively to the Legislatures of the Provinces; which exceptions are thus defined. in

Sec. 92, Sub-section 10:

a. Lines of Steam or other Ships. Railways. Canals, Telegraphs, and other Works and Undertakings connecting the Province with any other or others of the Provinces. or extending beyond the limits of the Province:

b. Lines of Steam Ships between the Province and any British or Foreign Country:

c. Such Works as, although wholly situate within the Province, are before or after their execution declared by the Parliament of Canada to be for the general advantage of Canada, or for the advantage of two or more of the Provinces.

Subjects under control of Provincial Legislatures.

Those which are placed under the exclusive control of the *Provincial Legislatures* are thus defined:

Sec. 92, Sub-sec. 10.—Local Works and Undertakings, other than such as form the exceptions above recited.

Sub-sec. 11.—The incorporation of Companies with Provincial objects.

Sub-sec. 16.—Generally all matters of a merely local or private nature in the Province.

It will be observed that the line of distinction is defined clearly with regard to certain classes of subjects only. Sub-section 10 empowers the Parliament of Canada to assume the control of any works wholly situate within one Province, that may be declared by that Body to be for the advantage of the Dominion, or of two or more Provinces. Two instances of this occurred in the first Session of Parliament, in the case of the Bill to incorporate the proprietors of the Ottawa and Prescott Railway, by the name of "The St. Lawrence and Ottawa Railway Company," and the Bill respecting the Northern Railway of Canada—in the enactment of each of which bills, Parliament declared that the Railway therein referred to was "a work for the general advantage of Canada."* The first mentioned bill contained a provision empowering the St. Lawrence and Ottawa Railway Company to build a bridge over the River Ottawa, and to construct a branch to Lake Deschesnes, in the Province of Quebec; but it was argued, in debate, that this would not in itself justify legislation by the Parliament of Canada, in reference to a Railway situate wholly within one Province, as it might afford a dangerous precedent to parties desirous of evading the jurisdiction of the Local Legislatures over works

Marginal notes: Works declared to be for the general advantage. St. Lawrence & Ottawa Railway. Northern Railway.

* 31 Vic., c. 20, sec. 1, and c. 86, sec. 2.

of a purely local character; and the course was adopted of introducing the clause above mentioned, in order to bring the bill properly within the jurisdiction of the Parliament of the Dominion.

All Railways intersecting Grand Trunk should be under same control.

These Railways are, thus far, the only ones of a local character that have been legislated upon by Parliament: but an impression would appear to prevail, that all Railways intersecting the Grand Trunk should be under the same Parliamentary control, to avoid the serious difficulties and inconveniences that might arise (so long as they are subject to a different jurisdiction) from conflicting regulations in reference to the running of trains, inspection of Railway, gauge, and other matters of detail.

Works extending beyond limits of a Province.

There is a class of Railways and other works included among those placed by section 92 (sub-sec. 10, *a*), under the exclusive control of the Parliament of the Dominion, that is referred to with some little ambiguity. The section reads " Lines of Steam or other ships. Railways, &c., connecting the Province with any other or others of the Provinces, *or extending beyond the limits of the Province.*" It is clear that the words "extending beyond the limits of the Province" cannot have been intended to apply to works merely connecting two adjacent Provinces, because they are described in the words immediately preceding. Nor, on the other hand, can they refer to any

Railway or other work actually extending into a foreign country, because, in the very nature of things, no such power of extension can be conferred by Canadian legislation. It would appear therefore that these words must have reference to such Railways, Telegraphs, or other works, as lead directly into a foreign country, such, for example, as the Great Western Railway, which connects directly with the United States Railway system, both at the Niagara Falls Suspension Bridge, and also at Detroit,—the Buffalo and Lake Huron Railway, connecting with United States Railways at Buffalo,—the Montreal and Champlain Railway, connecting at Rouse's Point with the Vermont Central, &c.

Several bills were passed by Parliament, in the Session of 1867-8, relating to works of this class, viz. :—To amend the Act for the incorporation of the North-west Navigation and Railway Co. (a Company empowered, among other things, to navigate Lakes Huron and Superior within the limits of Canada),—To confirm a By-law passed by the Directors of the Lake Memphremagog Navigation Company (whose steamers ply on a lake partly within the territory of the United States),—To incorporate the Clifton Suspension Bridge Co. (international),—and to authorize the carrying of gas pipes across the River Niagara, in order to facilitate the lighting of the Town of

Works of this class legislated on in 1867-8.

Clifton with gas (international). As none of these bills contained the "general advantage" clause, it may be assumed that the construction put by Parliament upon the provisions of the Imperial Act in regard to bills of this class agrees with that above suggested.

Companies for doing business throughout the Dominion.

There is another class of bills, concerning which serious doubts have arisen in regard to jurisdiction, namely, those for the incorporation of companies for the transaction of business of any kind *throughout the Dominion.* Sub-section 11 (above quoted) assigns to the Provincial Legislatures "the incorporation of companies with Provincial objects." In the first Session of the Parliament of the Dominion, several petitions were presented in reference to the incorporation. &c., of Insurance and other private companies. Upon two of these, praying respectively for the incorporation of the Gore District Mutual Fire Insurance Company, and of the Sorghum Growers' Association of the County of Essex, the Committee on Standing Orders (Commons) reported, in each case, that in their opinion the matter "came more properly within the jurisdiction of the Local Legislature of Ontario."* On the other hand, petitions for the incorporation of

* 5th and 8th Reports of Committee on Standing Orders (Commons). 1867-8.

the Merchants' Express Company of the Dominion of Canada,—for the incorporation of the Canadian Lake Underwriters' Association,—and for amending the Acts relating to the Canada West Farmers' Mutual and Stock Insurance Company, and changing the name to the Canada Farmers' Mutual Insurance Company, were reported upon favorably, and bills, introduced upon them, were passed, and became law.* Another petition, for an Act to grant certain powers to the Civil Service Building and Savings Society, was reported on favorably by the Standing Orders Committee of each House, and a bill introduced in the Commons. This bill was subsequently referred to the Committee on Banking and Commerce, who, after discussing, in committee, the question of jurisdiction, presented a report to the House, representing that "doubts had arisen as to whether the objects sought to be obtained by the promoters were not Provincial in their character, and such as the Local Legislature is exclusively empowered to deal with,"† and soliciting instruction on the subject. A similar proceeding took place on the part of the Private Bill Committee of the Senate, who presented a

---

* 31 Vic., chaps. 90, 91 and 93.

† 5th Report of Committee on Banking and Commerce (Commons), 1867-8.

report of a like nature in reference to a Bill to incorporate the Intercolonial Insurance Com-

Inquiry into ques-tion of ju-risdiction.

pany.* A discussion ensued upon the Report, which resulted in the appointment of a com-mittee " to inquire into and report to this House on the classes of Acts for the incorporation of private companies, which properly, under the ' British North America Act, 1867,' come within the jurisdiction of the Parliament of the Domin-ion, and to act on behalf of this House as Mem-bers of any Joint Committee of the Senate and House of Commons, which may be ordered on the subject." † No committee was appointed on the part of the Commons, and no further steps were taken with regard to either of the above mentioned bills.

Status of Provincial corpora-tions.

It was urged, on the part of the promoters of these bills, that the companies to which they related were desirous of transacting business in different parts of the Dominion, and were there-fore in need of more extensive and general powers than could be conferred upon them by a Provincial Legislature, and, in short, that they were not properly of the class referred to in Sub-section 11 of the Act, as "Companies with Pro-vincial objects." Against this it was argued that

* Report of Committee on Standing Orders and Private Bills (Senate), 5th Dec., 1867.

† Senate Journal, 12th Dec., 1867.

a Provincial Charter would suffice to ensure their recognition in every Province where their Agencies might be established; and that under such a charter they could sue and be sued, and transact all business of an ordinary character. In opposition to this view, a case was cited by the Honorable Mr. Campbell, in the debate in the Senate on the Bill to incorporate the Intercolonial Insurance Company, having an immediate bearing upon the question as to the *status* in one Province of a company incorporated by the Legislature of another Province. The case referred to was an action brought, in the Court of King's Bench of Upper Canada, by the Bank of Montreal, in the year 1836 (prior to the Union of Upper and Lower Canada), for the recovery of the amount of certain promissory notes, the drawers and endorsers of which resided in Upper Canada. The Court ruled that "a foreign corporation, such as a Bank, cannot maintain an action upon promissory notes received and discounted by them in the course of banking business in this Province, although they may maintain an action for money had and received to their use, against the person for whom such notes were discounted, and to whom money was advanced upon them."*

Case of Montreal Bank vs. Bethune, 1836.

* Bank of Montreal vs. Bethune, Hilary Term, 6 Wm. 4. (See Robinson & Harrison's Digest, p. 123.)

By this decision it would appear, that whatever *status* a company, owing its existence to a Provincial Charter, may possess beyond the limits of its own Province, there are limitations and restrictions which can only be obviated by special legislation in each Province. Banking Companies are, by the Act, placed under the exclusive control of the Parliament of the Dominion, and it may be found advisable, with a view of meeting the difficulty, that all commercial companies doing business of such a nature as to require the establishment of agencies in the different Provinces of the Dominion, should be placed under the same jurisdiction.

Foreign corporations in England and United States. Angell & Ames, in their " Treatise on the Law of Private Corporations aggregate," (6th edition, Boston, 1858,) shew (in treating on the powers of foreign corporations, s. 372), that " a company, claiming to be incorporated, has only to shew that it has been regularly and effectually made a corporate body, to enable it to sustain a suit beyond the jurisdiction within which it is constituted." They cite the case of the Dutch West India Company,—that of the National Bank of St. Charles, in Spain, and other analogous cases, in which it was decided by the English Courts, that a foreign corporation may maintain a suit in England by their corporate name. In the United States also, it is shewn (s. 373), that the power of a corporation to sue, in the respective States, is not restricted to companies created by the laws of the State in which the suit is instituted, but may be exercised by foreign corporations, belonging either to another State of the Confederacy, or to a foreign country. It is, however, admitted that this power is exercised rather upon sufferance than of right, as " the Legislature undoubtedly has power to prohibit foreign corporations (*i. e.*, those not created by the laws of the State) from contracting in the State ; but until it does so, contracts so made will be enforced." (s. 374.) But instances are given in which the powers of foreign corporations were restricted by the Courts without such Legislative intervention. In Ohio, the Court ruled (in *re* Bank of Marietta *vs.* Pindall), that "though, as a general rule, a corporation created by the laws of one State might sue in another, it would *not be permitted to a Bank in Ohio* to establish an agency in Virginia for discounting notes, or for carrying on any other banking operations; nor could they sustain an action on any note thus acquired by them," though they admitted " there was nothing in the policy of the laws of Virginia which restrained its citizens from borrowing money from a Bank in Ohio," &c. It was also held, by the Supreme Court of the State of New York, " that a foreign corporation, keeping an office in that State, for

Bank of Marietta in Ohio.

Decision of Supreme Court of New York.

receiving deposits and discounting notes, without being expressly authorized by the laws of that State to do so, *cannot maintain an action* for the money loaned."

These, it is true, are but rare and exceptional cases, yet they (with that relating to the Montreal Bank, before referred to), serve to shew that the powers of a corporation, beyond the territorial jurisdiction of the legislature creating it, are, in fact, exercised by permission rather than right, and are therefore subject to restriction or curtailment at any time. In considering what may be the true position of corporations created in this country under Provincial authority, it is well to bear in mind the very important difference that exists between the Constitution of the Dominion of Canada and that of the United States in regard to " State rights :" while, in the latter, the sovereignty of each State, in all matters of internal policy, is distinctly recognized and admitted, and all rights not expressly assigned by the constitution to the Federal Government are exercised by the Sovereign State,—under the constitution of Canada, the Sovereignty is expressly vested in the Government and Parliament of the Dominion, who have exclusive control over all matters not assigned exclusively to the Legislatures of the Provinces (British North America Act, sec. 91, class 29). This can hardly fail to have

[marginal note:] Difference between Constitutions of Canada and United States.

some effect upon the *status* of Corporations holding Provincial Charters, in any transactions they may have beyond the limits of their own Province. The Legislature of Ontario, at their first Session, in incorporating the Royal Canadian Insurance Company, expressly restricted their operations to risks "within the Province of Ontario." Insurance business, like that of Banks, is not confined to a particular locality, but is necessarily spread over the country, and the larger companies would probably desire to extend their operations over the greater part of the Dominion, and even beyond it (as regards Marine Insurance); it is therefore of importance to them that their corporate powers should proceed from the highest legislative authority in the land. A Bill respecting Insurance Companies,* passed in the first Session of the Parliament of Canada, requires all such companies to obtain a licence from the Minister of Finance, and to invest a large proportion of their paid-up capital in Dominion Stock, and contains other provisions for securing the proper management of the

Royal
Canadian
Insur. Co.
(Ontario)

Insurance
Companies.

---

* At one stage of this bill an objection was made, that it was beyond the jurisdiction of the House, which was over-ruled by Mr. Speaker; at another stage, a motion "that the regulation of Insurance Companies is a subject properly within the jurisdiction of the Provincial Legislatures," was proposed and negatived. Com. Journal, 1867-8, pp. 161, 426.

3

companies. This affords an additional reason
why it is desirable that Insurance Companies
should be created by the same authority that
exercises over them such stringent control.

In the first Session of the Legislature of Ontario
an Act was passed to incorporate the Guelph
Boards of Board of Trade. In the first Session of the Par-
Trade. liament of the Dominion, a bill was introduced
to incorporate the Stratford Board of Trade ; the
bill was referred to the Committee on Banking
and Commerce, and the question of jurisdiction
being raised in committee, the committee came
to the conclusion that though the Board to be
created was a local Board, the terms of the 91st
section of the " British America Act." in placing
" the Regulation of Trade and Commerce" under
the control of Parliament, justified the action of
this Legislature in the matter. In examining the
details of the bill, however, it was found to contain provisions for the establishment of a Court
of Arbitration in commercial matters ; and as
" the constitution, maintenance, and organization
of Provincial Courts, both of civil and criminal
jurisdiction," are, by the 92nd section of the said
Act assigned exclusively to the Provincial Legislatures, the committee expunged from the bill
so much as related to a Court of Arbitration, and
it was passed in the amended form.

It is much to be desired that steps should be

taken without delay to determine more accurately the question of jurisdiction, either by the action of the Canadian Parliament, or, if that be deemed insufficient, by invoking the interposition of the Imperial Parliament, to pass an explanatory Act.

As a preliminary step, it might be advisable to appoint a committee (upon which the various interests, Provincial and Dominional, should be duly represented), for the purpose of carefully considering the whole question of jurisdiction, and suggesting such amendments to the British America Act as may be found desirable, in order to determine doubtful points. Upon their report, an address to the Crown could be voted, soliciting the passage of an explanatory Act by the Imperial Parliament.

Another mode of meeting the difficulty has been suggested, viz.: that each bill upon which a doubt as to jurisdiction might be raised, should be discussed, and the point decided upon its own merits; and that in this manner a series of precedents would be established for future guidance. Not to mention other objections that might exist to this course, there is one that cannot be overlooked, viz., that the legislation of the Dominion Parliament cannot legally over-ride or interfere with the rights and privileges of the Provincial Legislatures, save in certain exceptional matters, as public works, and education; such powers as are vested in the Local Legislature being (with these exceptions) *exclusively* assigned to them, any proceeding or decision of Parliament upon a matter in any way exceeding its jurisdiction, instead of forming a precedent, will, in all probability, lead to the interposition of the Courts, and perhaps involve endless litigation. It is therefore of the utmost importance, that any attempt that may be made to deal with the question of jurisdiction, should be undertaken with due caution and deliberation.

4.—PARLIAMENTARY AGENTS.

In the Imperial Parliament, every private bill or petition must be solicited by a Parliamentary Agent, who conducts the bill through its various stages, and is personally responsible to the House and to the Speaker for the observance of the rules, orders, and practice of Parliament, and for the payment of all fees and charges : and no proceeding upon any petition or bill can take place, until an appearance to act as the Parliamentary Agent upon the same shall have been entered in the Private Bill Office.* This practice of employing Parliamentary Agents has been but recently introduced in Canada, and it has not hitherto been made obligatory, though the increase of business may possibly render it desirable to adopt some such course, in order that members may be relieved from a duty that is often inconvenient and embarrassing, and frequently involves a sacrifice of time and trouble, which should not in fairness be expected of them.

Parliamentary Agents must be employed in Imp'l Parliament

Not obligatory in Canada.

---

* May, p. 655.

In the revised code of Rules prepared by the late Sir Henry Smith (then Speaker), and adopted by the Assembly of 1860, provision was made for the recognition of Parliamentary Agents, **Mode of qualifying.** who had up to that time acted in a private and irresponsible capacity. No person is now permitted to Act as Parliamentary Agent, without the express sanction and authority of the Speaker.* This having been obtained, he is required to sign a declaration before the Chief Clerk of the Private Bill Office, engaging to observe and obey all the Rules of the House, and to pay all fees and charges, when demanded, and further, to enter into a recognizance in $2,000 (if required at any future time by the Speaker) conditioned to observe such declaration. His name is then registered in a book, and he is entitled to act as a Parliamentary Agent, but is liable to an absolute or temporary prohibition to practise (at the pleasure of the Speaker), for any wilful violation **Disqualif- cations.** of the Rules and practice of Parliament, or of any rules prescribed by the Speaker. Members†

72nd and
* ^73rd ~~and 74th~~ Rules, Commons.

† The House of Commons of Great Britain, by a Resolution of the 26th February, 1830, declared, *nem. con.*, " That it is contrary to the law and usage of Parliament that any Member of this House should be permitted to engage, either by himself or any partner, in the management of private bills before this or the

and Officers of the House* are alike disqalified
for Parliamentary Agency.

The name and place of residence of the Parlia- Registration of Agents.
mentary Agent soliciting a bill are entered in the
Private Bill Register, in which are also recorded
all the proceedings, from the petition to the passing of the bill. This book is open to public inspection.†

The Rules relating to Parliamentary Agents
belong only to the House of Commons, no regulations having been adopted by the Senate on this
subject.

It is usual for the Member who presents the Members in charge.
petition to take charge of the bill through its different stages.‡

---

other House of Parliament, for a pecuniary reward." Commons
Journ. (G. B.), 1830, p. 107.

One of the Sessional Orders of the Canadian House of Commons also declares "that the offer of any money or other advantage to any Member of the House of Commons, for the promoting of any matter whatsoever, depending or to be transacted in
the Parliament of the Dominion of Canada, is a high crime and
misdemeanor, and tends to the subversion of the Constitution.
Commons Journ., 1867-8, p. 5.

* In the Imperial Parliament, in compliance with the recommendation of a Select Committee on the House of Commons
Offices in 1835, no officer or clerk belonging to the establishment is allowed to transact private business before the House, for
his emolument or advantage, either directly or indirectly. May,
p. 656.

† The Rule.

‡ Sherwood on Private Bills, p. 29

5.—PETITIONS FOR PRIVATE BILLS.

Every Private Bill based on a petition.

Every private bill is based on a petition,* which should state, in general terms, the objects or privileges sought to be obtained by the parties soliciting the bill, and be signed by the parties themselves (the signatures of agents on behalf of others being inadmissable, except in case of incapacity by sickness); and at least one signature should be on the same sheet on which the petition is written.† The petition is presented by a

How presented.

Member in his place.‡ Petitions should be prepared in triplicate, one copy being presented in each House by a Member, and a third addressed to the Governor General in Council, through the Secretary of State. (A form of petition to each branch of the Legislature will be found in the

---

* 56th Rule. Bills relating to local improvements are occasionally brought in, in the Imperial Parliament, by order, without a petition, but are subsequently dealt with as private bills, as regards proof of compliance with standing orders, &c. May, p. 601.

† May, p. 509.

‡ 85th Rule, Commons.

Appendix, No. III.) In 1859 a Bill to incorpo- Bills which had not rate the Guelph and Wellington Roads Company, been based on a peti- was sent down by the Legislative Council, and tion. was subsequently referred to the Committee on Private Bills, who finding that it was not founded on a petition, reported that the preamble was not proved. In 1862, a Bill to separate the township of Broughton from the County of Megantic, and to annex it to the County of Beauce, which had been introduced as a public bill (under a public title), was referred to the committee, who reported that it was not based on a petition, and could not therefore be treated as a private bill; and no further proceeding was taken on the bill by the House.

The petition must be presented within the Time of first three weeks of the Session.* It was former- presenta- ly the custom to extend this time, by Resolution, tion. to a very late period of the Session, but the injurious tendency of such an extension has become so evident, from the necessity it frequently involves of dispensing with those formalities which are so necessary for the protection of private rights, that of late years there has been evinced an increasing unwillingness to extend the period. While in 1858, it was extended to 85 days from the commencement of the Session; in 1859 and

* 49th Rule.

1860. it was extended to 63, and in 1861 to 36 days only; the latter being but 15 days beyond the time fixed by the Rule. In 1867–8, an adjournment from December to March having been determined upon, the time for receiving petitions was extended to three weeks after the re-assembling of Parliament, and subsequently to the end of the then current month.

After expiration of time.

When the time has actually expired, parties are at liberty to present a petition, asking leave to introduce their petition for a private bill notwithstanding such expiry, and explaining the circumstances under which they have been prevented from complying with the orders of the House.* It is competent then to the House, either to grant the requisite permission upon motion,† or, in accordance with the practice in the Imperial Parliament,‡ to refer the matter to the Standing Orders Committee, and take action upon their report. In 1866, the House extended the time in favor of a particular application only.§

---

* Niagara Harbour and Dock Co., 1851; Randall Estate, 1852–3; Brockville and Ottawa Railway, 1863 (Feb. Sess.); Ottawa and French River communication, 1863 (Aug. Sess.) See also Sherwood on Private Bills, pp. 10, 23.

† Assembly Journ., 1852–3, p. 317; 1863 (Feb. Sess.), pp. 320, 326.

‡ May, p. 669.

§ Cobourg and Peterboro' Railway, 1866.

6.--PROOF OF NOTICES,

BEFORE COMMITTEE ON STANDING ORDERS.

All petitions for private bills, when received by the House, are taken into consideration (without special reference) by the Committee on Standing Orders, whose duty it is to ascertain whether the Rule of the House in regard to the publication of notice has been complied with in each case, and to report to the House the result of their inquiries; together with any recommendation that may appear to them desirable in cases where the notice may prove in any respect informal or insufficient.* The committee has no power to inquire into the merits of any such petition, this being a duty which pertains to the Private Bill Committee in considering the preamble of the bill.†

Examination of petitions without reference.

All private bills from the Senate (not being based on a petition already so reported on) are

Private Bills from Senate examined.

---

* 53rd Rule.

† Alpheus Todd's Report on Private Bills, 1847.

taken into consideration and reported upon by the
committee after the first reading.*

In 1862, the Legislative Assembly (in pursuance of a recommendation of the Standing Orders
Committee in their 10th Report) appointed the
Chief Clerk of the Private Bill Office their " Examiner for Standing Orders." assigning to him
the duty of examining into the facts with regard
to the notice given on each petition, and reporting the same for the information of the Committee
on Standing Orders: and the practice is continued under the new arrangements since Confederation. The committee are then enabled, upon
the evidence reported to them, to decide upon
each case. This corresponds with the course
taken in the Imperial Parliament :† it has been
adopted, as yet, only by the Lower House, and is
a step towards the assimilation of our Canadian
practice to that of the two Houses of the Imperial
Parliament for the joint proof of their Standing
Orders.‡

Marginal note: Examiner for Stand-ing Orders.

* 54th Rule. Toronto Boys' Home, 1861 ; Huron College,
1863 (Feb. Sess.); London and Canadian Loan and Agency Co.,
1863 (Aug. Sess.) ; Niagara District Bank, 1867-8.

† Bristowe, pp. 10, 77.

‡ In 1854 the Lords adopted a most convenient arrangement
which dispensed with a double proof of the Orders common to
both Houses; they resolved on the appointment of examiners for
Standing Orders for their Lordships' House, and appointed the

All questions arising in the committee are decided by a majority of voices; the chairman voting only when there is an equality of voices. In committees on private bills, the chairman votes as a member, and has also a second or casting vote when the votes are equal; but this power is specially conferred by a Standing Order of the House;* such is also the case in Election Committees, as regulated by statute; but as regards other committees, in the absence of any special power, it is contrary to the practice of Parliament.†

The Standing Orders Committee usually appoint certain days for sitting, in the Private Bill Office, when such petitions for private bills as have been received by the House, are laid before them. In cases where there is any doubt as to

Proceedings in committees

Sitting of committee.

---

same gentlemen who held the office of Examiners of petitions in the House of Commons, who were thus enabled to take the evidence on the part of both Houses simultaneously: and in cases where any of the Orders have not been complied with, the Standing Orders Committee in each House determines, upon the facts reported by them, whether the same ought or ought not to be dispensed with. "Of all the improvements," says May, "connected with Private Bill legislation, none have been so signal as those in which both Houses have concurred for the assimilation and joint proof of their standing orders." May, pp. 615, 616.

* 62nd Rule.
† May, p. 356.
‡

the sufficiency of the notice, the promoters of a petition appear before the committee, to produce such evidence as they may desire to offer.

Notices required in England. While the requirements of the standing orders of the Lords and Commons, relating to private bills, involve notices in various forms, and the depositing of plans, estimates. and other documents in some cases,* those of our Canadian Legislature (see Appendix I.) embrace (in all but Divorce cases) but one form of notice, *viz.*, by ad-*In Canada.* vertisement inserted in the *Canada Gazette*, and also in some newspaper published in any locality that may be affected by the proposed scheme, clearly and distinctly specifying the nature and object of the application : if the matter relate specially to the Province of Quebec it must be published both in English and French. This notice must be continued, not less than once a week, for a period of two months, during the interval of time between the close of the preceding Session and the consideration of the petition by the committee. In the case of a proposal to erect

---

* They are arranged in the following order :—1. Notices by advertisement. 2. Notices and applications to owners, lessees, and occupiers of lands and houses. 3. Documents required to be deposited, and the times and places of deposit. 4. Form in which plans, books of reference, sections and cross sections shall be prepared. 5. Estimates and deposit of money and declarations in certain cases. May, p. 611.

a toll bridge, the notice must state the rates of toll to be demanded, the extent of the exclusive privilege, the height of the arches, the interval between the abutments of piers for the passage of rafts and vessels, and, when it is intended to construct a draw-bridge, the dimensions of the same.*

When the application is for a Bill of Divorce, In Divorce cases. the notice is required by the Standing Orders of the Senate (see Appendix II.) to be published during six months in the *Canada Gazette*, and in two newspapers published in the District (in Quebec), or County or Union of Counties (in the other Provinces), where the applicant resides.† A copy of such notice in writing must also be served on the person from whom such Divorce is sought, if the residence of such person can be ascertained ; and proof on oath of such service (or of the attempts made to effect the same), must be adduced before the Senate on the reading of the petition.‡ An exemplification of all proceedings that may have been had in any Court of Law, duly certified, must be presented at the same time.§ And in all cases where damages have been awarded to the applicant, proof on

* 51st and 52nd Rules.

† 72nd Rule, Senate.

‡ 74th Rule, Senate.

§ 75th Rule, Senate.

74

oath must be adduced that such damages have been levied and retained, or such explanation afforded for the neglect or inability to levy the same under a writ of execution, as may appear sufficient excuse for such omissi n.*

Certain applications exempt from notice.   The various notices required by the Rules of the two Houses having been thus referred to, it should be mentioned that they do not apply to all applications for private bills, indiscriminately, but to such only as involve the granting of exclusive rights or privileges, or a possible interference with the rights or interests of other parties.† Thus petitions for the incorporation of religious. benevolent, social, literary, or educational institutions or associations,‡ for the naturalization of aliens,§ for some individual or personal advantage not of an exclusive charac-

* 76th Rule, Senate.
† 51st Rule (both Houses).
‡ Toronto House of Industry, 1852–3; St. Mary's College, 1852–3; German Evangelical Church incorporation, 1851–5; Canadian Order of Odd Fellows, 1856; Woodstock Literary Institute, 1857; Montreal St. Andrew's Society, 1858; Toronto Horticultural Society, 1860; Montreal Skating Club, 1861; Toronto Savings Bank, 1861; Montreal Natural History Society, 1862; Toronto Club, 1863; Humane Society of B. N. Am., 1864; St. Catharines Hospital, 1865; London Board of Trade, 1866.
§ Chaffee's naturalization, 1857; Stoeckel's naturalization, 1857. In the case of De Stoecklin's naturalization (1860), and

ter,* or for objects of a like nature, have usually been reported upon by the committee as exempt from the necessity of such notice; as have also applications for amendment of existing charters, when such amendment does not interfere with the rights of shareholders or others.†

Petitions have occasionally come before the committee, seeking certain powers or privileges, which, though not "exclusive" or directly involving (in the words of the 51st Rule) "any matter or thing which in its operation would affect the rights or property of other parties," might yet tend incidentally to affect the same. In such cases they have generally reported that notice was not required (under the terms of the Rule), but that provision should be made in the Bill for duly protecting all existing rights, &c.;‡ it then becomes

Provision in Bill, to supply want of notice.

Rogers' do. (1866), a suspension of the Rule relative to notice was recommended; and in those of Sanford and Rogers (1862) a Gazette notice was reported as sufficient.

* Mercer's relief, 1859; Poe's change of name, 1862; Ottawa Sisters of Charity (power to mortgage their property), 1863.

† Montreal Cemetery Co., 1852-3; Niagara Bank (extension of time for paying up stock), 1857; Eastern Townships Bank (reduction of capital), 1858; Port Whitby & Lake Huron Railroad Co. (do.), 1859; Toronto Cotton Mills Co., 1862; Jacques Cartier Bank, 1863; Merchants' Bank, 1864; Hamilton Board of Trade, 1866; London do., 1867-8.

‡ Platt Estate, 1858; Montreal and Champlain Railroad amendment, 1860; Guelph debt consolidation, 1860; Montreal Bank amendment, 1861, &c.

the duty of the Committee on Private Bills (or other committee of a like character), when the bill comes before them, to see that it contains such a provision, before they report it to the House.*

Evidence of publicity, when no notice is given.

In the fulfilment of their duty of examining into the notices given by the promoters of private bills in compliance with the 51st and 52nd Rules, the Committee on Standing Orders have generally been guided rather by the spirit than the letter of the requirement. In every case where the formal notice proves to have been insufficient, or to have been omitted altogether, they have admitted evidence to shew that all parties whose interests may be affected by the matter in question, have been fully informed of the intention to apply to Parliament. In admitting the propriety of such a distinction in the interpretation of the Rules, it must nevertheless be remembered that parties at a distance who may be aware of an existing informality, may be led to suppose that it will be fatal to the measure, and may therefore neglect to take any steps to oppose it, relying upon the House to carry out its own Standing Orders. This has, in fact, been the case in several instances, and a knowledge of it generally acts upon the committee in exercising their judgment as to the admissability of evidence of this kind. When the committee have become satisfied in this manner

* ~~54th~~ Rule.
53

concerning a notice thus technically defective or informal, they have in some instances taken upon themselves to waive the informality, and to report the notice as sufficient. Thus, publication of the proceedings at a public meeting called to consider a certain question, or some other public notice,* discussions in reference thereto in a City Council, reported in the local papers.† or service of notice on the shareholders of a company individually, or evidence of the knowledge or consent of parties affected.‡ have been held to be a sufficient substitute for the notice required by the Rule. They have dispensed with the local notice in a matter affecting a remote and unsettled part of the country,§ also, in the incorporation of Insurance Companies.‖ or Banks,¶ and in other

Informality waived, in certain cases.

---

* Three Rivers Diocese Church Rate, 1852-3 ; Joliette incorporation, 1863; Bruce County Town, 1864.

† Montreal Corporation amendment, 1856; Montreal City Passenger Railway, 1861; Toronto incorporation amendment, 1862; Quebec Corporation, 1864.

‡ Hamilton Hotel Co., 1856; Upper Canada Bank, 1862; Brockville & Ottawa Railway, 1863; Woodstock Literary Institute, 1864; Ottawa & Prescott Railway, 1865; McDougall Estate, 1865; Bruce By-law, 1866; St. Lawrence Tow Boat Co., 1866; Merchants' Bank, 1867-8.

§ Huron Copper Bay Co., 1849; Sault St. Marie Canal, 1852-3.

‖ British America Fire and Life Assurance Co., 1852-3, &c.

¶ Royal Bank of Canada, 1861, &c.

matters not affecting any particular locality.* They have also dispensed with notice in the Official Gazette in applications of a purely local nature,† and with the French local notice in a matter relating to the Eastern Townships of Lower Canada,‡ and the English local notice in one affecting a population of French origin.§

Suspension of Rule relative to notice.

The above cases must however be considered as altogether exceptional; while the committee may, in their discretion, interpret the Rules in the most liberal sense, they have no power to dispense with the formalities required by the House. When, after due examination, they consider it desirable to relax these formalities in any particular case, they report the facts to the House, and recommend a suspension of the Rule. The principal grounds upon which a suspension has been recommended may be thus stated:—Evidence of consent of parties interested, ‖ —That

* In companies of this nature, whose business is general rather than local, it is customary, when an amendment of their Charter is asked, to publish a local notice (in addition to that in the Official Gazette) in a newspaper circulating at the seat of their chief place of business.

† Iroquois School Section, 1858; Moulton Division, 1859; Cobourg Manufacturing Co., 1859: Burford Survey, 1860; Fitzroy Survey, 1863; Becancour Bridge, 1863; Fabriques Mutual Assurance, 1865.

‡ Iberville, Brome, Shefford, and Missisquoi Road, 1857.

§ Joliette Mining Co., 1857; Tring Municipality, 1863.

‖ Galt Estate, 1860: La Banque du People stock increase,

all parties have signed the petition,* —or are
sufficiently apprized of the application,† —That
the petition (in matters of a local nature) is very
generally signed,‡ —That no private rights will
be interfered with,§ —Proceedings in reference
thereto at a public meeting,‖ or in City Councils,¶
—That the notice will have fully matured
before any action can be taken on the bill by the

1861; Beauharnois Presbyterian Cong., 1861; Grand Trunk
Railway, 1862; Damble's relief, 1863; St. Thomas Debentures,
1864; McCallum's relief, 1865; Bar of L. Canada, 1866.

* Benson Estate, 1857; Cobourg Harbour Debentures, 1858;
N. Halifax boundary line, 1859; McKay's will, 1861; Kingston
Marine Railway, 1863; Iberville Academy, 1864; York
Roads, 1865; Aylmer Parish, 1866.

† London and Port Stanley Railway (sale of land), 1858;
Rouville division, 1859; Cobourg and Peterboro' Railway, 1862;
Saguenay Municipality, 1863; Montreal Corporation, 1865.

‡ Mitchell incorporation, 1857; Charlevoix Registry Office,
1858; Vespra and Sunnidale separation, 1859; Waterloo registration division, 1862; King Township Treasurer, 1863; Ya-
maska Bridge, 1864.

§ Woodstock Woollen and Cotton Manufacturing Co., 1860;
Northern Railway amendment, 1860; South Eastern Mining Co.,
1861; Huguenin's admission as notary, 1861; Crevier's relief,
1863; Knowlton Cemetery, 1865; Canadian Rubber Co., 1866;
Clifton Gas Works, 1867–8.

‖ Napanee incorporation, 1857; Cayuga Market block, 1863;
Port Hope By-law, 1865; Church of England Synod, 1866.

¶ Montreal incorporation amendment, 1854–5; Quebec
Police, 1857; Toronto Street Railway, 1861; Hamilton Debt,
1863.

Private Bill Committee.* —That the measure is one of great urgency.† or of great public utility or importance.‡ —That the notices were given for the previous Session, which was closed prematurely.§ —That Bank Charters have not heretofore been treated as private bills in New Brunswick,‖—and even, in one or two instances, on the ground that a petition had been presented against the proposed bill, which appears to have been considered as evidence that its opponents were sufficiently informed of the application.

In recommending a suspension of the Rule, however, when no sufficient notice has been given, the committee have suggested that certain matters of detail, which they considered to require notice, should not be included in the bill.¶

Up to the year 1856, it was occasionally the

---

* Durham separation, 1860; Petroleum Springs Road Co., 1861; St. Hyacinthe corporation, 1863; Lincoln County town, 1866.

† Hamilton debt consolidation, 1861; Oxford Seed Grain, 1863; Napanee Municipality, 1865.

‡ Transmundane Telegraph Co., 1859; St. Lawrence Navigation Co., 1861; North West Navigation and Railway Co., 1862.

§ Dereham Drainage, 1863; Niagara & Detroit Railway, 1865.

‖ Fredericton Bank, 1867-8.

¶ Stanstead, Shefford & Chambly Railway, 1863.

practice for the House to suspend, in a particular
case, the Rule relative to Notice, upon a motion
to that effect, without any previous action on the
part of the Standing Orders Committee; but in
that year the committee made a report, representing that the practice of indiscriminately dispensing with these notices must have a most
injurious tendency, and suggesting that in future
no motion for suspending the Rule in any special
case be passed, until the matter in question should
have been favorably reported on by the committee; this being acceded to by the House,
was acted upon for the remainder of that Session.
A similar recommendation made in the following
year, was modified by the House so as to provide
that no motion for suspending the Rule in favor
of any petition be entertained, until the committee shall have reported on the subject, favorably or otherwise; and this is now provided for
in the 55th Rule.

No suspension until committee has reported.

When, in any case, the notice, upon examination, proves to be insufficient, it is so reported to
the House, and (unless accompanied by a recommendation to suspend the Rule) all further action
in the matter is dropped; the decision of the
committee being rarely overruled by the House.*
One case is recorded in the Journals of the

Insufficient notice to be reported.

* May, p. 653.

Assembly. in which the committee having reported the notice incomplete, recommended that it be *not* dispensed with. The House nevertheless suspended the Rule, and referred the petition back to the committee. who subsequently reported favorably, and a bill was introduced.[*]

Notice must be specific and clear. In judging as to the sufficiency of a notice submitted for their examination, the committee compare its terms with those of the petition, and any important variance or omission in the former is fatal either to the whole measure. or to a particular provision therein, as the case may be. In some instances the notice (though published in the prescribed manner in other respects) has been unfavorably reported on because it did not sufficiently indicate the objects sought to be attained.[†] This was the case with a petition for an amendment to the Act incorporating the **Galt and Guelph Railway.** Galt and Guelph Railway Company in 1858; on examining the petition. the amendment was found to embrace a provision for giving the holders of certain bonds issued by the company before mortgaging their road to the Great Western Railway Company. a remedy against the last mentioned company. and this not having been mentioned in the notice, it was pronounced

---

[*] Huntingdon Plank Road Co., 1846.

[†] St. Lambert Municipality, 1861.

insufficient.* In another instance,† upon an application for amendments to the Act dividing Chatham into two municipalities, the notice simply referred to the Act, as 19 & 20 Vic., cap. 105, without mentioning the subject, and this was pronounced insufficient. In the same Session, the committee called the attention of the House (in one of their reports) to the utter insufficiency of a notice given in this form, and recommended " that in future, no notice be considered sufficient that does not clearly indicate the nature and subject of the application."‡ This recommendation has been acted upon by the committee ever since ; and in 1862 the (51st) Rule was so amended as to require every notice to be of this character. *Chatham division.*

If the notice be found too general in its terms, or if no mention be made of certain matters included in the petition which require a specific notice, the facts are specially reported, and the promoters restricted, in the details of the bill, *Petitioners restricted within the terms of the notice.*

---

* In a subsequent report, five weeks later, the commit'ee stated that the notice had since been amended, and advertised in its amended form for three weeks ; and they recommended that the Rule be suspended : this was done accordingly, and a bill presented, but it was not proceeded with.

† Chatham division, 1860. Also, Murray gravel roads, 1862 ; Colborne gravel roads, 1862.

‡ Assembly Journ., 1860, p. 126.

Exception. within the terms of the notice;* or if the matters
so omitted are allowed to be inserted in the bill,
due provision is made therein for the protection
of all parties whose rights might be affected by
the want of a specific notice.† If the notice
has been given in one County or District only,
the operations of the petitioners are confined to
that locality.‡

Peel Manu-
facturing
Co.

In 1865, in reporting on the petition of the
Peel General Manufacturing Company, for certain amendments to their charter, the committee
stated that the notice was sufficient for ordinary
amendments, but called the attention of the
House to one of a peculiar nature, under which
shareholders in the company might claim a
relaxation of the Patent Laws in favor of their
own inventions, when intended to be used in
connection with the company. The promoters
did not proceed with the bill.

In 1866, the County Council of Wellington,

---

* Port Hope Harbour, 1854-5; Vaudreuil Railway, 1854-5;
St. Lawrence and Bay Chaleurs Land Co., 1857; Brockville and
Ottawa Railway, 1860; Onslow Survey, 1862; Preston and
Berlin Railway, 1862; Joliette incorporation, 1863; Eastern
Townships Bank, 1861; De Léry Gold Mining Co., 1865; Long
Point Company, 1866.

† Montreal City Loan, 1862; Buffalo & Lake Huron Railway, 1863; Tadousac Hotel Co., 1865; Bank of U. C., 1866;
Clifton Suspension Bridge, 1867-8.

‡ St. Lawrence Mining Co., 1851-5.

having petitioned for an Act to legalize their By-law granting aid to a certain railway, presented a further petition, praying that the Rule requiring notice might be suspended in their case; and the Committee on Standing Orders, having considered the last mentioned petition, reported that no sufficient reason had been urged to induce them to recommend a suspension of the Rule. *(Wellington By-law.)*

In one case* the committee reported that the notice ought not to be dispensed with, but that a bill might be introduced for the relief of the petitioner, by extending in his favor the time for appealing against a decision of the Trinity Board. The bill was accordingly introduced, but was subsequently dropped. In another case† the committee reported that a charter proposed to be amended had become void by *non user*; and the House justified the report by taking no further action in the matter. *(Special Reports.)*

In the Session of 1867-8 (after Confederation), the committee reported, with reference to two petitions, that they appeared to come more properly within the jurisdiction of the Local Legislature,‡ and they were not proceeded with

---

* Malcolm Smith, to be reinstated as a pilot, 1859.

† North-west Transit Co., 1861; and again in 1862.

‡ Gore District Mutual Insurance Association, 1867-8; Sorghum Growers' Association of Essex, 1867-8.

(See also chapter on Legislative Jurisdiction, *supra*, p. 13.)

Other parties cannot avail themselves of a notice. It may be well to state, that the committee (though not reporting any such case to the House) has repeatedly decided that parties having a diverse interest from those by whom a notice has been published, cannot avail themselves of such notice to proceed upon their own account; among other cases, this decision was given in regard to the Sault Ste. Marie Canal in 1851, and Gage's Will case in 1862, to the knowledge of the writer.

Petitions referred back. After an unfavorable report from the committee, the House has, in a few instances,[*] referred petitions back to the committee, with an instruction to consider and report as to the expediency of suspending the Rule. In one case only[†] was their report favorable; and though in this instance the Rule was suspended, and a bill introduced, it was subsequently abandoned.

Further Report, amending a former one. It has occasionally happened, that after certain petitions have been unfavorably reported on, further evidence has been produced, sufficient to satisfy the committee. In such cases they have made a further report, amending the former one, and representing either that the notice has since

---

[*] Reach road allowance, 1856; Elora incorporation, 1856; Turner's contract on Brant Gaol and Court House, 1856.

[†] Elora incorporation, 1856.

been continued so as to complete the full time
required,* or that it has been amended so as to
meet the requirements of the Rule,† or that the
evidence subsequently adduced proves that the
notice was sufficient for all parties concerned.‡

---

* Hamilton & Amherstburg Railway, 1854-5; Peterborough
School Trustees, 1857; St. Bonaventure Municipality, 1866.

† Galt & Guelph Railway amendment, 1858.

‡ British Farmers' Union Insurance Co. of Brantford, 1859.

7.—PRESENTATION AND FIRST READING OF BILL.

Presenta-tion of Bill.

When a petition has been favorably reported on by the Committee on Standing Orders, a bill may be introduced, upon a motion for leave. ~~upon a Monday, Wednesday or Friday, immediately before the calling of the Order for private bill,*~~ (preceded, when the same is required by the Report, by a motion to suspend the Rules). The bill must be prepared by the promoters, in the English and French languages, and printed (at their expense) by the Parliamentary contractor; ~~and~~ 600 copies in English and 200 in French,† ~~must be deposited in the Private Bill Office,~~

of which must [be filed with] the House & for the [use of] Printing.

---

* 56th Rule, Commons. Members of the Senate exercise the right of bringing in bills, in that House, *without* a motion for leave, in analogy with the practice in the House of Lords. May, p. 439.

† Formerly, such bills only as related to Lower Canada were required to be printed in French, but in 1867 this Rule was made to apply to all bills. The printing of the French version was occasionally dispensed with in bills concerning some locality within the Eastern Townships of L. Canada.—St. Francis Bank, 1851-5 ; Eastern Townships Bank, 1851-5.

~~and distribution thereof made before the first~~ *Read*
~~reading.* It is only in the House of Commons,~~
however, that bills are required to be printed at
this stage, in conformity to the Rule adopted in
1867. In the Senate they are printed, as hereto-
~~fore, before the second reading.†~~

The amount of any rates, tolls, fees or fines
inserted in the bill, must be printed in *italics*;
these are technically regarded by the House as
blanks, to be filled up by the committee on the
bill, and are so inserted merely to shew the
amount intended to be proposed.‡

When a bill for confirming any letters patent
or agreement is presented, a true copy of the
same must be attached thereto.§ A bill of
this kind having been referred to the Private
Bill Committee in 1857, they reported that they
could not recommend that it be passed, because
no copy of the letters patent was attached. The
omission was, however, rectified by the House, a
copy of the letters patent being attached to the
bill in committee of the whole, and it finally
received the Royal Assent.‖

In 1864, several petitions relating to munici-

Rates and tolls to be in italics.

Bills for confirming any letters patent, or agreement.

* 58th Rule, Commons.
† ~~55th Rule, Senate.~~
‡ May, p. 670.
§ 57th Rule.
‖ Bessemer's Patent, 1857.

Provisions of several petitions included in one bill. palities within the same district, having been favorably reported on, the provisions of legislation sought by the different petitioners, were combined into one bill by the promoters.*

Bills informally introduced. If a bill has been informally or irregularly introduced (*i.e.*, prior to the presentation of a petition, or to the Report of the Standing Orders Committee on such petition), it may be withdrawn, with the leave of the House, and a new bill be presented in the proper course.†

Time of presentation. Private bills must be presented within the first four weeks of the Session :‡—but this period is generally extended, to correspond with a like extension in favor of petitions. (See *supra*, p. 33.)

Reference to a standing committee, in Commons. Every private bill, when read a first time, in the House of Commons, is referred to the Standing Committee on Private Bills, the Standing Committee on Banking and Commerce, the Standing Committee on Railways, Canals, and Telegraph lines, or some other Standing Committee of a like nature : and all petitions for or against the bill§ stand referred to such com-

* Arthabaska and Wolfe Municipalities, 1864.

† Halifax Townships, 1859 ; Rouville Division, 1859 ; Chicoutimi Municipality, 1863 ; Union St. Joseph, Three Rivers, 1865.

‡ 49th Rule.

§ Petitions in favor of, or against private bills, are not presented in the House of Commons in the usual way of presenting

mittee. No bill,* originating in that House, of
which notice is required to be given under the
51st Rule, can be considered, after such reference,
until after ~~in clear days~~ ' notice of the sitting of
the committee, affixed in the lobby, and appended
also to the Votes. In the case of bills received
from the Senate, the notice required is ~~two days~~
only.† Bills not requiring notice under the
51st Rule may be considered at any time after
reference.

~~This is another of the changes effected in 1867;~~
it was adopted with a view to expedite the proceedings on private bills, and to enable the committees to enter at an earlier period upon their
labors, and so avoid the accumulation of business
too often thrust upon them near the close of the
Session. In the Senate, the practice in relation
to the reference of bills (which, until that year,
was identical in both Houses), remains as heretofore; bills are not referred until after the *second*
reading,‡ and the notice to be given by the
~~committee is one week, upon bills of the Senate~~,

Reference
to a Stand-
ing Com-
mittee, in
Senate.

---

petitions, but are deposited in the Private Bill Office; and all
such as are deposited within a certain time after the second
reading of the bill, stand referred to the committee. May, p. 653.

* 59th Rule, Commons.
† 60th Rule, Commons.
‡ ~~79th Rule, Senate.~~

~~and 24 hours upon the ——— ut up from the Commons.~~ *

Divorce Bills.   Divorce Bills (which invariably originate in the Upper House) are referred (after their first reading in the Commons) to a selected committee, in place of the Standing Committee on Private Bills.† The evidence taken before the Senate (a copy of which is applied for, and communicated, by message) is referred to the committee, with power to send for persons and papers, and usually, to hear counsel.‡ The committee give ~~two~~ *the* days' notice of their sitting, as in the case of other private bills.

* ~~40th Rule, Senate~~.

† In the British House of Commons, they are referred to " The Select Committee on Divorce Bills." May, p. 758.

‡ Harris' divorce Bill, 1844–5; Beresford's do., 1852–3; McLean's do., 1858; and again in 1859.

8.—PAYMENT OF FEE AND CHARGES.

Immediately after the ~~first reading (or, in the Senate, after the~~ *second reading*), and before the consideration of the bill by the committee, the fee and all other charges thereon, must be paid ~~into~~ *accordingly* ~~the Private Bill Office~~. This however applies only to bills "giving any exclusive privilege, or for any object of profit, or private, corporate, or individual advantage; or for amending, extending or enlarging any former Acts in such manner as to confer additional powers." On all such bills a fee of $100 is levied, and the promoters are charged with the expense of printing 600 copies of the bill in English and 200 in French, and of printing 500 copies of the Act in English and 200 in French, with the Statutes: this last item is subsequently refunded if the bill should fail to become law.* If the bill has not been prepared in both languages, it is charged with the cost of translation; and any additional expense incurred, for re-printing the bill in an amended form, or for printing sched-

Fee payable after first reading.

Limitation

---

* 58th Rule.

PAYMENT OF FEE.

Fee payable in one House only.

ules of tolls or other papers connected therewith, must be defrayed by the promoters. The Fee is payable only in the House in which the bill originates, and the charges for printing are made in the House in which they may be incurred. On Divorce Bills (which originate in the Upper House) the fee of $200 must be deposited in the hands of the Clerk of the Senate at the time of presenting the petition.*

Formerly the amount of the Fee charged on private bills was $60. In 1854-5, the Standing Committee of the Assembly on Contingencies reported a recommendation that the amount should be increased upon all private bills to $200; † and in 1862, the Committee on Private Bills reported‡ in favor of a scale of fees, adopting the existing rate ($60) as the *minimum*, and charging two rates on bills for raising or expending a sum amounting to $200,000 and under $400,000,—three rates when amounting to $400,000 and under $600,000, and so on in proportion ;—but no action was taken by the House on either Report.§ In

* 34th Rule, Senate.

† Assembly Journ., 1854-5, p. 358.

‡ 18th Report of Committee on Private Bills, L.A., 1862.

§ In the British House of Commons, every bill " for the particular benefit of any person or persons" is deemed a private bill within the meaning of the Table of Fees; and a fee is charged at each stage of the proceedings on the petition and bill, of like

the codes of Rules adopted by the Senate and
House of Commons in 1867, the amount of the fee
was raised to $100. *and in 1874 to $200.*

In a few instances the fee has been refunded Refunding
upon the recommendation of the Private Bill of fees.
Committee, on the ground that the bill was abandoned by the promoters,*—that it amends an
Act of the present Session on which the fee was
already paid,†—that the fee was paid in the previous Session,‡—that the bill was rendered
necessary by the legislation of the previous Session,§—that there were legal difficulties in the
way of its passing,‖—that the bill has been laid
aside, and a general Act substituted,¶—or that
the amendments to the charter of a certain

---

amount in all cases, except that when the amount to be raised or
expended is £50,000 and under £100,000, the fees payable at
the 1st, 2nd, and 3rd readings (£45 in all) are doubled,—if between £100,000 and £200,000, they are tripled,—and so on in
proportion. Fees are also paid by the opponents of a bill, on
presenting a petition against it. Bristowe, pp. 135 to 137.

* St. Lawrence Mining Co., 1852-3 ; Galt & Guelph Railway, 1866; Toronto and Owen Sound Railway, 1866; North-
west Transportation Co., 1866 ; Canadian Mutual Life Insurance
Co., 1867-8.

† Guelph lands trust, 1854-5.

‡ Johnston Estate, 1864.

§ Coyne's relief, 1865.

‖ Ayr dam and water-course (J. Watson), 1856.

¶ Various bills for admission of attorneys to practise, 1857.

G

company, were rather for the advantage of the
public than of the company.* More frequently
the fee has been refunded without the recommendation of the committee, by a motion to suspend the Rule, though the attempt has not always been successful. It has been customary,
upon the rejection or abandonment of a bill, to
refund the fees, upon a special motion being made
to that effect in the House,—but one instance of
a refusal to refund the same having occurred.†
The fees have even, in some instances, been refunded at a subsequent Session.‡

Recommendation of committee required. In 1863, a recommendation of the Committee
on Private Bills, that for the future, no motion for
remitting the fee upon any bill be entertained, except upon the recommendation of the
committee,§ was concurred in by the House;
and it has since been generally acted upon.

Proceedings continued to another Session. The Spring Session of 1863 having been brought
to a premature close, before the private business
could be completed, such of the bills (on which
the fees had been paid) as were re-introduced at
the next Session were exempted from any further
payment.‖ Arrangements were also made, in

* Provincial Insurance Co., 1858; U. & L. Canada Bridge
Co, 1864.

† Lake Superior Mining Co., 1852-3.

‡ Bank of Canada, 1865 (Aug. Sess.); Quebec Pilots, *ib*.

§ Assembly Journ., 1863 (Feb. Sess.), p. 210.

‖ Assembly Journ., 1863 (Aug. Sess.), pp. 91, 93.

the same Session (Autumn Session of 1863), by
which, in case that Session should be suddenly
closed, all private and other bills undisposed of
at the prorogation should, at the beginning of the
next Session, be at once advanced to the stage at
which they had been suspended;* and a like
arrangement was effected in the Spring Session
of 1865.†

---

* Assembly Journ., 1863, pp. 282, 283.
† Assembly Journ., 1865 (Jan. Sess.), pp. 223, 216.

9.—COMMITTEES ON PRIVATE BILLS,

AND THEIR POWERS.

Standing committees on private bills.

It has been already stated that all private bills before the House of Commons are referred, after the ~~first~~ reading, either to the Standing Committee on Private Bills, or to that on Banking and Commerce, or that on Railways, Canals, and Telegraph lines, or to some other Standing Committee of a similar character.* These committees are appointed early in the Session, and continue in existence until its close.† They each consist of a large

---

* In 1866, the Bill respecting the Bar of Lower Canada was referred to a *select* committee.

† This differs from the practice in the Imperial Parliament, where all railway and canal bills before the Commons are referred, after the *second* reading, to the "General Committee on Railway and Canal Bills," and all other private bills to the "Committee of Selection." The bills are classified in groups by these committees, who severally nominate special committees to consider each group, with one of their own members as chairman. (May, p. 674.) Each member of the committee on an opposed bill is required to sign a declaration that his constituents have no local interest, and that he has no personal interest in the bill, &c. (*Ib.*, p. 682.)

number of members, who are nominated by a committee of selection (for all standing committees), and the nomination confirmed by the House. At their first meeting they proceed to elect a chairman. The quorum consists of a majority of the members, though of late years it has been customary for each committee, after its organization, to make a report recommending a reduction of the quorum,* which has been concurred in by the House. Members may be subsequently added by the House.

Instructions may be given to these committees by the House, concerning particular bills, or other matters.† After referring a bill, the House may, if it think proper, instruct the committee to report it back before consideration.‡ The Private Bill Committee have themselves occasionally reported back bills which they thought might more advantageously be referred to another committee.§ The notice already given by the committee under the 60th Rule, has generally been declared, in such

Special Instructions.

---

* In 1859, and in each subsequent Session (up to 1867, inclusive), the quorum of the Private Bill Committee was, in this manner, reduced to *seven* members, while that of the Railway Committee was, in the Sessions between 1857 and 1861 inclusive, reduced to *nine*, but has since that time consisted of a majority of the members.

† May, p. 722.

‡ Isle Jésus Roads Co. ; Terrebonne Roads Co., 1863 (Feb. Sess.); Napanee River Improvements Co., 1866.

§ Niagara District Bank, 1863.

cases, sufficient.* The Standing Committee on Railways was, in 1852-3, instructed to consider the expediency of amending the bill for empowering the Great Western Railroad Company to construct a railroad from Hamilton to Toronto, so as to authorize them to construct a branch railway from their line to Port Dalhousie, and they reported the bill with an additional clause providing for the said branch.† The committee was again instructed in 1854-5, to enquire into the expediency of establishing a branch telegraph in the Parliament House; which was subsequently effected, upon their report.‡ In 1863, the Standing Committee on Banking and Insurance, having under consideration a bill to repeal the Acts incorporating the Colonial Bank and certain other Banks that had forfeited their charters, made a report suggesting that they be empowered to extend their inquiries to any other banks in a like position; and they were instructed accordingly.§ There are some general instructions given by Standing Orders of the House, concerning all private bills, viz. :—to call the attention of the House to any provision that does not appear to have been contemplated in the notice, as reported on by the Committee on Standing

Special instructions.

General Instructions.

---

* Assembly Journ., 1863 (Feb. Sess.) p. 176; 1866, p. 202.
† Assembly Journ., 1852-3, pp. 290, 340.
‡ Assembly Journ., 1854-5, pp. 177, 197, 229.
§ Assembly Journ., 1863 (Aug. Sess.), p. 102.

Orders ;*—to require proof in every case that the persons whose names appear in a bill for incorporating a company are of full age, and in a position to effect the objects contemplated, and have consented to become incorporated.† And in bills for confirming any letters patent, or agreement, the committee is required to see that there is a true copy of the same annexed to the bill.‡ Certain specific instructions are given by Standing Orders of the Houses of Lords and Commons, to committees on all Railway Bills,§ the object of which is, no doubt, to a certain extent attained in this country by the provisions of the General Railway clauses consolidation Act. There are also certain general instructions on all bills relating to Inclosure and Drainage, Turnpike Roads, Cemeteries and Gas Works, and Divorce cases.‖

The committee has no power to entertain questions in reference to the compliance with the Standing Orders,¶ (which pertains solely to the Standing Orders Committee) unless by special order from the House. This order is only given when the House, on the report of the Standing

No power
to inquire
into Standing Orders.

* 63rd ~~64th~~ Rule.
† 615 ~~642nd~~ Rule.
‡ 57th Rule. See also May, pp. 713, 714.
§ Bristowe, p. 23.
‖ Bristowe, p. 26.
¶ Sherwood, p. 46.

Orders Committee, allow parties to proceed with their bill on complying with certain standing orders which they had previously neglected.*
In ordinary cases the committee merely inquire whether the Orders of the House have been complied with; and in cases where a special report has been made by the Standing Orders Committee in reference to the extent of the notice, it is compared with the powers and privileges conferred by the bill, and if they appear to exceed the limits of the notice, the fact is specially reported to the House.†

Bill must agree with the notice proved.

Examination of witnesses upon oath.

The committee has power to send for persons and papers, and to examine witnesses upon oath, the expenses of such witnesses being defrayed by the parties in whose interest they have been summoned. Prior to Confederation, the committees of either House had no power to examine witnesses upon oath, several attempts to pass a law to confer such a power having failed; ‡ but in the Session of 1867-8, an Act was passed empowering the committee on any private bill, in either House of Parliament, to examine witnesses upon oath, to be administered by the chairman or any member of such committee.§

---

* May, p. 707.
† 64th Rule.
‡ Assembly Journ , 1856, pp. 498, 503, 559; and 1857, pp. 31, 191.
§ 31 Vic., c. 24, sections 2 and 3.

In all questions arising before the committee, Casting vote of chairman. the chairman votes as a member, and whenever the voices are equal, he has a second or casting vote.* This provision was introduced in the revised code of Rules adopted in 1860, and is expressly limited to committees on private bills (including the Standing Committee on Private Bills, and that on Railways, and any other committee to whom private bills may be referred): it is based on Imperial practice.† The Controverted Elections Act of Canada confers the same power on the chairman of an election committee.‡

Every member present in the committee should Every member should vote vote on all questions brought up, judging from the analogy of the practice of the House in this respect,§ and that of Election Committees under the provisions of the above mentioned Act, though in the absence of any express rule or order it may be questioned whether the committee has power to compel a member to vote who declines to do so.‖

---

* 62nd Rule.

† This practice prevails in committees of the Commons on private bills; but in the Lords' Committees the chairman votes like any other peer; and if the numbers on a division be equal, the question is negatived. May, pp. 386, 387.

‡ Consol. Stat. of Canada, Chap. 7, sec. 89.

§ May, p. 331.

‖ Frere has some excellent remarks upon this question; but

Cannot sit during sitting of the House.

The committee cannot sit during the sitting of the House; all proceedings are void after announcement that the Speaker is in the Chair.* Leave has, however, in two instances, been granted to the Committee on Private Bills to sit during the morning sittings of the Legislative Assembly,—once in 1858,† for one occasion only, and again, in 1860,‡ for the residue of the Session.§

the difference in the constitution of committees on private bills in the House of Commons, renders these remarks less applicable to the Standing Committees on private bills in this country. Frere, p. 75,—and again, on p. 81.

* Sherwood, p. 45.

† Assembly Journ., 1858, p. 658.

‡ Assembly Journ., 1860, p. 311.

§ By a Standing Order of the House of Commons of Great Britain, 21st July, 1856, it is ordered "That on Wednesdays and other morning sittings of the House, all committees shall have leave to sit, except while the House is at prayers, during the sitting, and notwithstanding the adjournment of the House." And to avoid interruption to urgent business before committees, leave is frequently obtained, on the meeting of the House in the afternoon, for a committee to sit till 5 o'clock. May, p. 388.

10.—PROCEEDINGS IN COMMITTEE ON BILL.

At each sitting, a list of the bills which are ready for consideration is laid before the committee, in the order of their reference; and they are usually taken up in that order, unless it may be otherwise agreed upon, for the convenience of parties in attendance. In the case of opposed bills, it is customary for the parties to come to an arrangement in the Private Bill Office for the selection of a particular day for the consideration of a bill in which they are interested; and the bill, in such a case, takes precedence of all other bills appointed for that day: where no such arrangement is made, the bill is taken up in its order. It has been stated above, that no bill of which notice by advertisement is required by the Rules, can be considered until due notice has been given by the committee.* This notice is

Order of consideration.

Notice given by committee in certain cases.

---

* This notice consists, in the Commons, of ~~10 days~~ one week (affixed in the Lobby, and appended to the Votes), upon bills originating in that House, and 2 ~~days~~ hours upon bills from the Upper House. (60th Rule, Commons.) In the Senate the notice

frequently reduced by the House, towards the
close of the Session, to 2 or 3 days;* but no
motion to this effect (of a general nature) can
now be entertained by the House, except upon
the recommendation of two or more of the Standing Committees charged with the consideration
of private bills.† In some instances it has been
dispensed with altogether, upon special motion, as
regards particular bills;‡ the propriety of this
course, however, has been much questioned, on
the ground of the wrong inflicted on parties who
may desire to oppose any such bill, and for whose
protection this notice is intended; and a suspension
of the Rule in this behalf is now less frequent, being
made only in urgent cases.

Parties desirous of opposing any bill before a

must be one week (affixed in the Lobby) on bills originating in
that House, and 24 hours upon bills from the Commons. (60th
Rule, Senate.)

* Assembly Journ., 1857, p. 423; 1858, p. 907; 1859, p.
271; 1860, pp. 232, 311; 1861, p. 216; 1865 (Aug. Sess.),
pp. 108, 175; 1866, p. 117.

† 60th Rule.

‡ Colonial Bank, 1858 ; Oshawa incorporation, 1859 ; Peterboro' and Victoria land tax, 1860 ; London Church land, 1863
(Aug. Sess.), on the recommendation of the committee, at
the request of all parties. And on the 28th May, 1862, the
Rule was suspended altogether for the residue of the Session.
In 1863 (Aug. Sess.) it was suspended with reference to all
bills which had been reported on in the previous Session, which
had closed prematurely.

committee, either on the preamble or the details, Opponents should present a petition. present a petition, stating the grounds of their opposition.* No such petition can be entertained that does not distinctly specify the grounds on which the petitioners object to the bill or any of its provisions. The petitioners can only be heard on the grounds so stated, and if the same are not specified with sufficient accuracy, the committee may direct a more specific statement to be given in writing, but limited to the grounds of objection which had been inaccurately specified.† No petitioners will be heard against the preamble, unless in their petition they pray to be heard against it.‡ If no parties, counsel, or agent, appear on behalf of a petition when it is And fyle appearance.

---

* In the Commons of Great Britain (as has already been stated) all petitions in favor of, or against, or otherwise relating to private bills (except the original petition for the bill, and petitions for additional provisions), are now presented by depositing them in the Private Bill Office. Every petition against a private bill, deposited not later than 10 days after the first reading, stands referred to the committee. Petitioners will not be heard before the committee unless their petition has been prepared and signed in strict conformity with the rules and orders of the House, and has been deposited within the time limited, except where they complain of any matter which may have arisen in committee, or of any proposed amendment, or additional provision. May, pp. 685, 686.

† May, p. 687.

‡ Bristowe, p. 28.

7

read, the opposition of the petitioner is held to be abandoned.* It is right, however, to state, with regard to these restrictions, that although strictly speaking they apply to all opposed bills, they are never fully enforced by the committee, unless the circumstances of the case appear to require it.

Counsel.

The promoters of a bill may be heard by counsel if they desire it.† Petitioners against the preamble or any of the clauses may be heard by counsel, if, in their petition, they have prayed to be heard by themselves, their counsel, or agent.‡ No member can act as counsel before the House or before any committee; nor can any member of either House act as counsel before the other House, on any bill depending therein, without special permission: when such permission is given, it is understood that the gentlemen who receive it would not be permitted to vote on

To what extent members may act.

* Bristowe, p. 27.

† A Parliamentary Agent appearing before a committee of the British House of Commons for a private bill (or upon a petition against a bill containing a prayer to be heard by counsel) is always called on by the committee clerk to hand in the names of two counsel, though the number of counsel who may be heard is not limited to these.—Evidence of G. L. Smith, Esq., Parliamentary Agent,—appended to the 3rd Report of the Committee of the House of Commons on Private Bills, 1847. (Ans. to Ques. 913.)

‡ Standing Orders of British House of Commons relative to Private Bills, 85.

such bill, if it should be received by the House
of which they are members.* This permission
has in a few instances been given to members of
the Assembly,†—and once only to a member of
the Legislative Council.‡

~~A filled up copy of the bill, containing the~~ Filled up
amendments proposed to be ~~submitted~~ by the Bill to be
promoters, must be ~~deposited~~ in the Private Bill fyled.
Office, one ~~clear~~ day before the consideration of
~~the bill.~~§ All parties petitioning against the
bill are entitled to obtain a copy of the proposed
amendments, one day before the consideration of
the bill.‖

In the case of the Quebec Marine Insurance Amend-
Co. in 1865 (Jan. Sess.), a petition was presented, ments by
on the part of the company, for leave to amend promoters
their bill in a matter not contemplated by the

---

* May, p. 358.

† Leave was granted by the Legislative Assembly to the
Hon. T. C. Aylwin, in the session of 1844-5, to appear at the
Bar of the Legislative Council on the Naturalization Bill
(Donegani's),—and to Messrs. Ross and Cauchon, in 1850, on
the Dorchester Bridge Bill. Assembly Journ., 1844-5, p. 408;
1850, p. 261.

‡ Leave was granted by the Legislative Council, in 1843,
to the Hon. Mr. Draper, to appear at the Bar of the Legislative
Assembly as Counsel on the bill relating to the University of
Toronto. Council Journ., 1843, p. 101.

~~§ 61st Rule.~~

‖ May, p. 682.

notice. and the Standing Orders Committee reported favorably on the petition, on the ground that the sanction of the shareholders to the amendment had been obtained. A like course was taken in regard to the Montreal Corporation bill, in the autumn Session of the same year.

Preamble read.

When the committee are about to proceed to the consideration of a private bill, the parties are called in, and the preamble is read; this being different from the practice in regard to public bills. the preamble of which is postponed until after the consideration of the clauses.* (Instances may. however, arise, in which the committee may feel it desirable that they should reserve their judgment upon the preamble until certain details of the bill have been settled: in such a case they postpone the preamble until after the consideration of the clauses; but this is of very rare occurrence.) The petitions against the bill are then read, and appearances entered

---

* This course is adopted in regard to public bills, because they are founded on reasons of state policy, and the House having affirmed the principle on the second reading, it becomes the duty of the committee not to discuss the principle again upon the preamble, but to settle the clauses first, and then to consider the preamble in reference to the clauses only. (May, p. 468.) But the expediency of a private bill being mainly founded on the allegations of fact (contained in the preamble) proof of such allegations is necessary, as a proper basis of legislation. (Ib. p. 718.)

upon each petition with which the parties intend
to proceed.*

The promoters (or their counsel) first state their case on the preamble, and then (if required) proceed to call witnesses, and to examine them. At the conclusion of this examination, when the counsel or agent for any petitioner rises to cross-examine a witness, is the proper time for taking objections to the *locus standi* of such petitioner.† It is necessary that a petitioner should state the manner in which his interest is affected, in order that he may obtain a *locus standi* at all in opposition to the measure ; but the grounds of objection to the bill on which he may be heard in support of such opposition, are not confined to those arising immediately out of his private interests.‡

If the committee decide in favor of his *locus standi*, he may address the committee, and produce his witnesses, and they in their turn are cross-examined by the counsel for the promoters, who has the right to reply.§ The committee may, if they please, hear petitioners against a bill on the ground

Side note: Promoters heard.

Side note: Locus standi of petitioners.

---

* May, p. 716.

† Petitioners are said to have no *locus standi* before a committee, when their property or interests are not directly and specially affected by the bill, or when, for other reasons, they are not entitled to oppose it. May, p. 690.

‡ Frere, p. 32.

§ Bristowe, p. 23.

Petitioners against a bill. of competition;* but shareholders of a company promoting a bill are not heard in opposition unless their interest be distinct from that of the company.†

A petitioner whose interest is affected only by particular clauses in the bill, which are immaterial to the main objects of the measure, and are not referred to in the preamble, would have no right to be heard against the preamble, but only against such clauses.‡

Members required as witnesses. If the attendance of a member of the House be required as a witness, the proper course is for the chairman to write to the member requesting his attendance; if he refuse to attend, the fact is reported to the House, in order that they may take such steps in the matter as they see fit.§

Expenses of witnesses. A witness has a right to claim that his expenses be paid or guaranteed, before his examination. A witness cannot correct his evidence, except by a subsequent examination.‖

---

* May, p. 695.
† May, p. 699.
‡ Frere, p. 33.
§ Frere, p. 70. A Peer of Parliament cannot be compelled to attend a committee of the Commons, but if he attend voluntarily, it is not necessary that a message be sent to the Lords requesting his attendance, as is the case in committees on public matters. *Ib.*, p. 71.
‖ Frere, p. 72.

When counsel are addressing the committee, or while witnesses are under examination, the committee room is an open court; but when the committee are about to deliberate, all the counsel, agents, witnesses, and strangers are ordered to withdraw, and the committee sit with closed doors. When they have decided any question, the doors are again opened, and the chairman acquaints the parties with the determination of the committee, if it concern them.* {.marginnote: Room cleared for discussion.}

Members of the House who are not on the committee, have a right to be present during the examination of witnesses, but not to interfere in the proceedings.† It is doubtful how far the committee has a right to exclude them from the room when cleared for discussion, but it is always customary for them to retire. {.marginnote: Right of members of the House to be present.}

If any member insist on his right to remain, against the wish of the committee, their only course is to report the circumstances of the case to the House.‡ If a member of the House be under examination as a witness, and the matter under consideration shall have arisen out of his {.marginnote: A member under examination.}

---

* May, p. 715.

† By a Standing Order of the House of Lords, all Peers are entitled to attend the select committees of that House, and they are not excluded from speaking (though they be not of the committee), but they may not vote. May, p. 382.

‡ Frere, p. 74.

evidence, the right of the committee to exclude him from the room during the discussion, is less doubtful.*

Question put on preamble. When the arguments and evidence upon the preamble have been heard, the room is cleared, and a question is put " That the preamble has been proved," which is resolved in the affirmative or the negative, as the case may be: † —If in the negative, the committee report to the House " That the preamble has not been proved to their **Preamble not proved.** satisfaction." After this decision, it is not competent for the committee to re-consider and reverse it, but the bill should (if necessary) be re-committed for that purpose.‡

In the Imperial Parliament, the committee are

' The India Judicature Committee (House of Commons), in 1782, having cleared the room to deliberate on the refusal of Mr. Barwell to answer certain questions, he insisted on his privilege, as a Member of the House, of being present during the debate. The committee objected that as a party concerned in the matter under discussion, he had no right to be present. Mr. Barwell still persisting in his right, two members attended the Speaker, and returned with his opinion that Mr. Barwell had no right to insist upon being present during the debate, upon which he withdrew. The House subsequently ordered " That when any matter shall arise on which the said committee wish to debate, it shall be at their discretion to require every person not being a member of the committee to withdraw." May, p. 332.

† May, p. 720.

‡ May, p. 722.

not required to assign any reasons for thus de-
ciding against the further progress of the bill,
though the necessity for such information, to enable the House to determine upon their report, is
obvious.* A different course prevails in Canada,
the committee being required to state in their re-
port† the grounds of their decision. Of these
may be instanced,—That no evidence was offered
in favor of the preamble, ‡ —Insufficient information or contrary evidence, § —No proof (in the
petition or otherwise) of consent of the parties interested, ‖ —No proof that the majority of those
whose interests would be affected are in favor of
the scheme,¶—That the petitioners against the
measure are as numerous as those in its favor,**
or are more numerous,††— That there is great

Reasons assigned.

---

* Alpheus Todd's Report on Private Bills, 1847.

† 66th Rule.

‡ River du Chêne, 1852–3; Gatien estate, 1857.

§ Small's Pickering road allowance, 1852–3; Clarke Survey, 1857; Notre Dame du Portage Municipality, 1859; Onslow
Survey, 1862.

‖ Bill to incorporate the Benevolent Societies of the Wes-
leyan Church, 1850; Guelph and Welling'on Roads Co., 1859;
Russel Estate, 1865.

¶ Hull Presbyterian Church, 1856; Quebec limits extension, 1860; Lennox and Addington separation, 1860.

** Whitby division, 1857; Stanbridge division, 1866.

†† Grey and Simcoe division, 1857; Bolton incorporation,
1858; Durham School section, 1859; Berlin town limits, 1865.

difference of opinion in the locality affected, as to
the expediency of the measure,* —That the statement of facts set forth in the preamble has been
disproved,† —That legislative interference is not
desirable or necessary.‡ —That it would interfere with law-suits pending,§ or with existing
rights,‖ —That the powers sought for would not
advance the interests of the locality.¶ —That the
bill provides for an extension of the powers of a
certain company to purposes entirely foreign to
its original charter,** —That it contains most unusual provisions,†† —That a certain survey

---

* Ayr incorporation, 1857; Halifax township, 1860; Clifton division, 1866.

† Barton road allowance, 1852–3.

‡ East Hawkesbury survey, 1856; Clarke survey, 1856;
Van Norman estate, 1857; Delaware survey, 1857; York and
Peel separation, 1861 ; Quebec Stevedores incorporation, 1861 ;
Augusta Municipalities' Fund, 1862; Bruce county town, 1861 ;
Bayham by-law, 1865, and 1866 ; Montreal Licensed Victuallers,
1865.

§ Chatham survey, 1858; Peel county town, 1859: Rich-
mond Street (London) boundary line, 1861; Peterboro' and
Port Hope Railway, 1862.

‖ North-western Railway, 1856; Clifton suspension bridge,
1858; Burford survey, 1860; Hope survey, 1860; Etchemin
bridge, 1862; Renfrew division, 1863.

¶ St. Lawrence and Bay Chaleurs Land and Lumber Co., 1858.

** St. Clair and Rondeau Plank Road Co. amendment, 1857.

†† Metropolitan Gas and Water Co., 1857; Richelieu Company, 1862.

which is sought to be confirmed was not made in conformity with the provisions of the law, * — Preamble not proved That the filled-up bill submitted to the committee differed materially from the printed bill as originally referred to them, and was not in accordance with the petition,† —or, That it is in the power of the Executive Government to carry into effect the objects contemplated by the bill,‡ or the Court of Chancery (in a bill affecting the interests of minors).§ In one instance, in 1857, the committee reported, with reference to the bill to incorporate the St. Lawrence and Bay Chaleurs Land and Lumber Co., that although they could not say the preamble was not proved, yet they could not recommend the passing of the bill, its promoters being foreigners, residing out of the Province.

If, upon the report of the committee concerning Committee may be required to report evidence which guided their decision. a certain bill, that the preamble is not proved, the House be not satisfied with the reasons assigned in the report, the committee are directed to report the reasons or evidence which guided them in their decision ; and these, when reported, have generally satisfied the House, so that the bill has

* Beverly survey, 1864.

† Toronto Esplanade, 1851-5.

‡ Bill to vest in J. Carling and others, a portion of Church Street, London, 1852-3.

§ Watson's Ayr Mill-dam, 1856.

Bill may be referred back for amendment. proceeded no further.* If it should appear from the report, that the objection to the bill was not so much against the principle as against certain details, the committee may be instructed to amend the bill by striking out the objectionable provisions, and report the same as amended.† In one instance, however, they reported that a majority against the preamble had been obtained through one member having voted against it inadvertently; and the instruction of the House having afforded him an opportunity of correcting his vote, he had done so, and this having given a majority in favor of the preamble, the committee reported the bill.‡ In other cases, the committee having been directed to report the evidence on which their adverse decision was founded, reported the same, and it was referred to a committee of the whole, with the bill, and the bill was reported and passed.§

Alterations in preamble. It is in the power of the committee to make alterations in the preamble,‖ either by striking out or modifying such allegations as may not have

---

* Cornwall By-law, 1856; Metropolitan Gas and Water Co., 1857; St. Lawrence and Bay Chaleurs Land Co., 1858; Peterboro' and Port Hope Railway, 1862.

† Richelieu Company, 1862.

‡ Three Rivers diocese church-rate, 1852-3.

§ Clarke survey, 1857; Bruce County town, 1861.

‖ May, p. 723.

b..en substantiated to their satisfaction, or by ex-
punging such as the promoters may be desirous Alterations
in preamble
of withdrawing ;* but no new allegations or
provisions ought to be inserted, either in the preamble or the bill, excepting such as are covered
by the petition and the notice, as proved before
the Standing Orders Committee,—unless the parties have received permission from the House to
introduce such additional provisions, in compliance with a petition for leave.† Every material alteration in the preamble must be specially
reported to the House, with the reasons therefor.‡
Such alterations have almost invariably hitherto
been of a nature to limit or reduce the powers
proposed to be conferred by the bill.§ An exception was made, however, in the case of a bill
for the relief of the Ministers of a certain religious
denomination in Montreal, in 1857,‖—the preamble and provisions of which were amended so
as to apply to all ministers of that denomination
in Lower Canada; and it was passed in the

---

* Sherwood, p. 53.

† May, p. 721. See also 64th Rule.

‡ 65th Rule.

§ St. Hyacinthe incorporation, 1852-3 ; Upper Canada
Mining Co., 1852-3; Toronto Bank, 1854-5; Frelighsburg
Grammar School, 1857 ; St. Gabriel de Valcartier division, 1861;
Renfrew By-law, 1863.

‖ Bill for relief of Ministers of the Church of the "Countess
of Huntingdon's Connexion" at Montreal, 1857.

8

amended form. (But see the remarks as to the limitation of the power of the committee to make amendments, on p. 91.)

"Previous Question" cannot be put. It is a rule of Parliamentary practice, that the "previous question" cannot be put in committees, i.e., that if the question were proposed that the preamble is proved, it is not competent for a member to propose the previous question "that that question be *now* put," for the purpose of voting against it. The same rule applies, of course, to the clauses, and to any amendments proposed.*

Preamble proved. When the committee have decided that the preamble has been proved, they call in the parties, acquaint them with the decision, and then go through the bill, clause by clause, and fill up the blanks; and when petitions have been presented against a clause, or proposing amendments, or for **Proceedings on clauses.** compensation, the parties are heard in support of their objections, or amendments, or claims, as they arise. Clauses may be postponed, and considered at a later period in the proceedings, if the committee think fit; or clauses which the parties have agreed to insert in the bill may, if necessary, be produced before the committee decide on the preamble.† Manuscript clauses are con-

* May, pp. 361, 473; Frere. p. 49.
† May, p. 720; Bristowe. p. 29.

sidered after those printed in the bill, first those proposed by the promoters, and afterwards such as may be proposed by the opponents of the bill.* If any unusual provisions are found in the bill, or any that do not appear to have been contemplated in the notice, special mention is to be made of them in the report.† *Unusual provisions.*

In the case of any bill sent down from the Senate, the committee, if they have not sufficient evidence before them, can direct their chairman to move in the House that a message be sent to their Honors, requesting that the proofs and evidence on which the bill was founded may be communicated; and these, when sent down, are referred to the committee.‡ *Evidence on bills from Senate.*

In filling up the blanks in the bill, the committee are required to insert the maximum rates of toll, fees, or other charges to be imposed under its provisions, which are printed in the bill in *italics*, for the information of the House, but are technically regarded as blanks.§ A practice obtained occasionally, for some years, of requiring the rates of toll proposed to be inserted in *Rates of toll or fees.*

---

* Frere, pp. 54, 61.

† Montreal Building Society; Montreal Gas Co.; Toronto Dry Dock; various Mining Bills: all in 1847. See also 64th Rule.

‡ Counter's stove patent, 1850; Niagara and Detroit Rivers Railroad, 1859; Quebec Pilots, 1860.

§ May, p. 670.

Rates of
toll, &c.

Harbour. Bridge, or Canal Bills, to be first sanctioned in a committee of the whole, and afterwards referred to the committee on the bill for insertion therein. This appears to have been the usual course prior to the Union, but upon the adoption of a system of Private Bill legislation, it was discontinued. In the Session of 1852–3, this practice was resorted to in a bill to incorporate the Port Burwell Harbour Company,* and was subsequently observed in several instances; though it was always the exception rather than the rule. The inconvenience of this practice is most evident, as it is manifest that the committee of the whole can, at that early stage of the bill, have no sufficient evidence to guide them in establishing the rates of toll; while on the other hand, the committee on the bill have it in their power to procure all necessary information : when they report the amended bill, it is referred (after the second reading) to a committee of the whole, and an opportunity afforded to the House of exercising its judgment in the matter. Moreover tolls of this kind are imposed only upon such persons as may voluntarily use the works to be constructed under the authority of the bill, as a fair equivalent for a service rendered. and are thus altogether different in their character from a com-

---

* Assembly Journ., 1852–3, pp. 269, 285.

pulsory rate, duty, or charge upon the people, Rates of toll, &c. which should undoubtedly originate in a committee of the whole.* Furthermore, while the rule, as regards rates, duties, etc., inserted in public bills, is strictly observed in the Imperial Parliament, all private bills are exempt from its operation, including even those under which a local rate is proposed to be levied for a local work.† In 1862, the Committee on Private Bills presented a report, recommending that the exceptional practice referred to be discontinued,‡ and the recommendation has since been generally acted upon.

The amendments made by the committee are Amendments reported to the House. written upon a printed copy of the bill, which is signed by the chairman, who also signs, with his

---

* Three Rivers Diocese Church Rate, 1852-3.

† In 1833, a committee of the Commons (G. B.), appointed to examine into precedents in connection with this subject reported "that the general spirit of the Standing Orders and Reso- "lutions of the House, requires that every proposition to impose "a burthen or charge on any class or portion of the people, "should receive its first discussion in a committee of the whole "House. The only exception from this rule is with regard to "*tolls, rates, or duties* proposed to be levied on the subject in "*particular places* for any *local work;* and in such cases it is "directed that no bill be ordered to be brought in till the peti- "tion for it has been referred to a committee, and they have ex- "amined the matter thereof, and reported the same to the "House." May (edition of 1844), p. 275.

‡ 18th Rep. of Com. on Private Bills, L. A., 1862.

or attached to the Report.

Amendments reported to the House.

initials, each amendment made, and clause added, and another copy of the bill as amended is fyled ~~in the Private Bill Office~~.* The committee, in reporting the bill, call the attention of the House to any provision that does not appear to have been contemplated in the notice,† or to any provision of an unusual character,‡ and if they have amended the bill in such a manner as to confine its provisions within the terms of the notice,§ or otherwise to restrict the same,‖ it is usually mentioned in the report. It is customary also to make special mention of any amendment of a peculiar or unusual character. as. changing the name of a proposed corporation,¶ —extending the limits of a township proposed to be erected,** —or materially altering certain arrangements provided for by the bill.†† In 1858, the

---

* 5th Rule.

† 63rd Rule. See also Three Rivers Corporation, 1861.

‡ Quebec Pilots' Corporation, 1866.

§ Middlesex debt, 1854-5.

‖ Toronto and Goderich Railway. 1851; London debt, 1856; Martin's Saltfleet road allowance, 1856; Fitzroy Survey, 1863.

¶ Canadian Life and Fire Insurance Co., 1856; Colonial Bank, 1856.

** Franklin Township, 1857.

†† London town lot (Agricultural Societies), 1856; Crowland Survey, 1862; BelleIsle's relief, 1863; Foley's admission as Barrister, 1864.

committee reported a bill to detach certain lots in the township of Barton from the city of Hamilton, which they had so amended as to provide for continuing the lots in question within the limits of the city at a limited rate of taxation; they also reported a bill to provide for the separation of the Counties of Durham and Northumberland, amended in such a manner as to leave the question of separation, &c., to the decision of the reeves and deputy reeves of the County of Durham. In 1864, they amended a bill to erect the Local Municipality of St. Colombe into a County Municipality, in such a way as merely to extend the powers of the said municipality in regard to the issuing of tavern and shop licences. *Special amendments.*

The power of the committee to make amendments is, however, limited; care must be taken in preparing them, that they involve no infraction of the Standing Orders, and are not excessive.* No new provisions may be intro- *Limitation of power to make amendments.*

---

* May, p. 681. Questions have frequently arisen (in the Imperial House of Commons) as to the right of a committee on a Railway Bill to alter the plan, which under the Standing Orders is required to be deposited in the Private Bill Office. The rules and practice of Parliament recognize this power, but the committee, before adopting any deviation from the line delineated on the plan, require proof of the consent of the owners or occupiers through whose property the proposed deviation will pass. Sherwood, p. 57.

duced by which the interest of parties who are
not suitors to the bill, or petitioners before the
committee, can be affected, without due notice
having been given to such parties.* If the com-
Material
alterations. mittee consider a material alteration desirable in
a particular bill (of such a nature as appears to exceed their powers), they report the bill, and suggest
such alterations as may meet the supposed necessity.† In 1852–3, a bill to incorporate the Mutual
Insurance Association for the Fabriques of the
Diocese of Quebec, was reported, with a recommendation that the principle should be extended
to each Diocese in Lower Canada; and the bill
was amended accordingly, and passed. In 1860,
in reporting on a bill to incorporate the Annuity
and Guarantee Funds Society of the Bank of
Montreal, the committee expressed their opinion
that it was advisable to make it a general measure,
applicable to any other Bank and its employés.
The suggestion was not, however, adopted by
the House, and the bill was proceeded with and
passed, as a private bill. In some cases, where
the committee have considered an amendment of
the general law preferable to the passage of pri-

* Frere, p. 61.

† B. N. American Mining Co., 1847; Bill to remove the
Registry Office for the County of Terrebonne, 1847. In this
last mentioned case, a division of the county for registration
purposes was suggested, instead of a removal.

rteason

nrt

vate acts, they have made a special report to that effect, and (occasionally) postponed the consideration of the bills to which it had reference, to afford an opportunity for the action of the House in the matter;* or, in other cases, they have expunged certain provisions, and recommended an amendment of the general law in these respects.†

In 1867–8 (after Confederation), the question of jurisdiction having been raised before them with regard to certain bills, they in one case ‡ solicited an instruction from the House, which, not being given, the bill was not proceeded with: in two other cases § they amended the bills and reported them, calling attention, in their report, to the doubts raised ; one of these bills was subsequently proceeded with, and the other abandoned. (See Chapter on "Legislative Jurisdiction," *ante*.) The committee have nothing to do with the title of the bill, which is only agreed to by the House after the third reading.‖

---

* Various bills for the admission of English attorneys to practise in Canada; also various bills for incorporating Mining Companies, 1854-5. (No action was taken on the reports, and the consideration of the bills being subsequently resumed, they were reported and passed.) Joliette incorporation, 1863.

† Kingsey Falls Municipality, 1864; DeLéry Gold Mining Co., 1865 ; Quebec Corporation, 1865.

‡ Civil Service Building Society, 1867–8.

§ Stratford Board of Trade, and Canada Live Stock Insurance Co., 1867–8.

‖ Frere, p. 66.

Power to divide or to consolidate bills.

Power may be given to the committee by the House to divide a bill into two bills, or to consolidate two bills referred to them into one.* This last has sometimes been done by the committee, without a special Instruction.†

Abandonment of a bill by its promoters.

Every bill referred to the committee must be reported.‡ If the promoters of any bill inform the committee that they do not desire to proceed further with it, the fact is reported to the House,§ and the bill will be ordered to be withdrawn :‖ or if any other parties before the committee, either as petitioners or opponents of the bill, desire to proceed with it, the committee may permit them to do so.¶ In 1867–8, the Committee on Banking and Commerce reported, with regard to a bill to incorporate the Canadian Mutual Life Insurance Co., that the principle of mutual life

---

* Frere, p. 65.

† St. Albert de Warwick Municipality, 1863. (In 1861 several petitions relating to municipalities in Arthabaska and Wolfe, were combined into one bill by the promoters.)

‡ 64th Rule.

§ St. Lawrence Mining Co., 1852–3; Ottawa Water Works, 1866; Galt and Guelph Railway, 1866; Toronto and Owen Sound Railway, 1866; North-west Transportation Co., 1866.

‖ May, p. 726.

¶ The Manchester and Salford improvement Bill, in 1828, was abandoned in committee by its original promoters; when its opponents, having succeeded in introducing certain amendments, undertook to solicit its further progress. May, p. 633. (Note.)

insurance being new to this country, they could
not recommend its adoption unless a paid up
guarantee capital of at least $50,000 was pro-
vided: and as the promoters were not prepared
to do this, they had abandoned the bill.

A bill, after it has been reported, may be referred **Bill may be referred back.**
back to the same committee,* or to some other
committee† but this is very rarely done.

The evidence taken by the committee is not **Evidence not reported, without an order.**
generally reported to the House, except in those
cases where a special order to that effect may be
made;‡ it is entered in a book, with the minutes
of the proceedings of the committee, and kept in
the Private Bill Office; but in some instances the
committee have reported their proceedings without an order being made.§

If the amendments made by the committee are so **Bill may be re-printed.**
important or extensive as to render it necessary that
it should be reprinted before its consideration by the
House, this is done at the expense of the promoters.‖

* Maskinongé Common, 1852-3; Strathroy and Port Frank
Railway, 1857; Streetsville incorporation, 1858; Lindsay, Re-
serve, 1859; Hamilton debt, 1863 (Aug. Sess.): St. Colombe
Municipality, and other bills, 1864.

† Canadian Land and Emigration Co., 1865 (Jan. Sess.);
Ashley's naturalization, ib.

‡ Great Southern Railway, 1857. See also supra, p. 83.

§ Buffalo and Lake Huron Railway, 1856; Grand Trunk
Railway, 1862; Montreal and Champlain Railroad, 1864.

‖ This is required in all cases, in the Imperial Parliament,
when the bill is amended. May, p. 728.

Time for
reports
limited.

The 49th Rule, while it limits the time for receiving petitions and private bills, respectively, also provides that no report of any standing or select committee upon a private bill be received after the first six weeks, but this period is invariably extended until nearly the close of the Session.

11.—SECOND READING OF BILL.

By the 65th Rule of the House of Commons, all private bills reported from a standing committee are placed on the Orders of the Day following the reception of the report,* for consideration ~~second reading~~, next after bills referred to a committee of the whole House,—though they are usually taken up only on "Private Bill" days; the only exception being in the case of bills on which the committee have reported the preamble not proven, which are not placed on the Orders of the Day at all, unless by special order of the House.

Time for second reading.

The second reading corresponds with the same stage in other bills, and in agreeing to it the House affirms the principle of the measure.† There is an important distinction between public

Principle of bill confirmed at this stage.

---

* In 1861, and in several subsequent Sessions, the committee, in reporting certain bills at a late period of the Session, recommended that they be placed on "the Orders of this day," which was done accordingly. Assembly Journ., 1861, p. 293, &c., &c.

† May, p. 456.

9

and private bills at this stage of the proceedings; a public bill being founded on reasons of public policy, the House, in agreeing to its second reading, accepts and affirms those reasons; but the expediency of a private bill is mainly founded upon allegations of fact, to be proved before a committee. It was formerly the practice, in each House, to refer the bill *after* the second reading; the affirmation of the principle of the bill, therefore, was necessary conditional, being contingent upon satisfactory proof being made of the allegations of the preamble. In 1867, the House of Commons changed their Rule in this respect, and provided for a reference of the bill after the *first* reading,*—the second reading being postponed until after the committee had reported. By this arrangement the House is put in possession, before the second reading, of the facts of the case, and is therefore in a position to deal with the bill upon its merits. ~~This change has not been adopted as yet, by the Senate, and bills before that House are referred, as heretofore, after the second reading.~~†

Recent change.

Hearing of Counsel.

The usual time for counsel to be heard at the Bar of the House upon a bill (*pro* or *con*.) is at the second reading; but opposition has rarely been offered, hitherto, at this stage, unless upon the assumption that the principle of the proposed

---

* 59th Rule, Commons. {This Rule was again changed in 18 , and the Bill is now referred after 2nd reading;}

~~† 59th Rule, Senate.~~

measure was objectionable on grounds of public policy.* Upon four occasions only, in Canada, has counsel been heard at the Bar against the second reading of private bills.† In one instance, ‡ the House resolved (upon petitions from the parties) to hear counsel, for and against the bill, upon the question for going into committee of the whole thereon : this having been (under the arrangements then in force) the first opportunity afforded for the action of the House after the report of the committee, corresponded, in point of fact (as regarded the time for hearing opposition) with the second reading under the new arrangement. The bill having been reported by the committee with amendments, they were directed to report the evidence, and the same was printed, with the bill in its amended shape. The Order of the Day for the House in committee on the bill, being read, counsel was called in and heard: it

---

* Sherwood, p. 37. The Street Rail Com'y Bill was thrown out on the second reading, in the British House of Commons, 16th April, 1861, on notice being taken that it trenched on public rights. In England it is the duty of the Chairman of Committee of Ways and Means, under a standing order, to call the attention of the House to all such cases. Hansard's Debates, vol. 162, p. 641.

† University of Toronto (King's College) Bill, (a Ministerial private bill), 1843, 1844-5, and 1846; Montreal Consumers' Gas Co., 1846.

‡ Great Southern Railway, 1857.

was then moved " that this House will resolve itself into the said committee on this day three
months:" the consideration of this motion was
postponed, and the bill was subsequently abandoned. It may be here observed, that a motion
to postpone the consideration of a bill for three
or six months, offered at any stage, is, if agreed
to, equivalent to a rejection of the bill for that
Session.*

Private Bills on the Orders of the Day, in the
House of Commons, are called up on Mondays,
immediately after the daily routine of business;
on Wednesdays and Fridays they are called for
the first hour, at the evening sitting; while on
Tuesdays and Thursdays they do not appear on
the Orders at all.† Private Bills in the hands
of members of the Administration, are placed
among the "Government Orders" on Government
days (Tuesdays and Fridays). In the Senate, no
days are specially appointed for the consideration
of private bills, but they come up from day to day,
according to their relative position upon the
Orders of the Day.

*Private
Bill days,
Commons.*

*are placed on the
list on the Orders*

---

* May, p. 673.
† 19th Rule, Commons.

12.—PROCEEDINGS IN COMMITTEE OF THE WHOLE.

All Private Bills, after ~~the second reading~~ report, are at once referred to a committee of the whole House, for consideration on some future day.[*] Several bills may be considered in committee at the same time.[†] *Reference to committee of whole.*

Counsel may be heard at the Bar of the House, at this or any other stage,[‡] but the usual time is at the second reading. (See Remarks on this subject, under "Second Reading of Bill," *ante*, p. 98.) *Hearing of Counsel.*

It may be well to remark here, that while it is, of course, competent to the House to amend or

---

[*] This differs from the practice in the Imperial Parliament, where such private bills as are reported without amendment are ordered for a third reading; while those reported with amendments are referred to the Chairman of Ways and Means, and the Speaker's Counsel, to report whether (in their amended form) they contain the provisions required by the Standing Orders, &c. May, p. 729.

[†] May, p. 467. Also, Assembly Journ., 1860, p. 445; 1861, p. 319; 1863 (Aug. Sess.), p. 173; 1864, p. 373; 1865 (Jan. Sess.), p. 231; 1866, p. 195.

May, p. 460.

reject any bill after it has been reported by a select
committee, and to amend or reject any of the
amendments agreed to by the committee, practically this right is rarely exercised. The inability of the House to discuss a private bill upon its
merits in the absence of such information as evidence alone can supply, renders its reference to a
select committee indispensable; and the House
practically delegates its responsibility to that committee, and almost invariably accepts their decision. The principle thus acted upon by our
Canadian Legislature, has been established in the
Imperial Parliament as the result of a very long
experience in private bill legislation. The Right
Hon. John E. Denison, Speaker of the House of
Commons, a very high authority in all matters
connected with either public or private Parliamentary business, in his evidence before a committee of that House upon the Business of the
House, in 1861, says, in reference to this question,—" If you look at the precedent of private
" legislation, you will see that some few years ago
" it was held that it would be quite impossible to
" concede such enormous interests as railway in-
" terests to a committee of five men; but these
" enormous interests, such as the consolidation of
" all the railways in the centre of Scotland, which
" was discussed before the House of Commons the
" other day, and the great question of the docks at

" Liverpool and the Mersey, now go to five men
" appointed by the Committee of Selection, and
" practically there is no appeal from their decision,
" because the House has been obliged almost to
" adopt as a rule that it will not interfere with the
" decision of committees."* In a subsequent
part of his evidence, after re-iterating this statement, he adds, that the House is more disposed
to support the decision of the committee, because
the smallness of the number of the members in-
creases the responsibility of the committee.†

In pursuance of this principle, the practice has
prevailed of late years, in the Lower House, in
the consideration of private bills in committee of
the whole, of not treating the amendments made
by the select committee as amendments, but considering the bill, as amended, as a whole; thus in
reporting the bill to the House, the chairman re-
fers only to the amendments made in committee of the whole. Bills from the Senate form
a necessary exception to this practice, as every
amendment made to the bill as sent down from
that House must be communicated for its concurrence.

Amendments of committee in committee of the whole.

Before the House resolves itself into committee
on a bill, an instruction may be given to the com-

* Report from the Select Committee of the House of Commons, on the business of the House, 1861. (Ans. to Ques. 155.)
† Same Report. (Ans. to Ques. 183 to 186, 192.)

Instructions to committee of whole.

mittee, empowering them to make provision for any matters not relevant to the subject matter of the bill. An instruction is not ordinarily *compulsory*, but rather *permissive*; a mandatory or compulsory instruction may, however, be given, and instances are to be found in which committees on bills have been instructed "that they do make provision," &c., or "do make two bills into one."[*] An instruction should always be made a distinct question, after the order of the day has been read, and not as an amendment to the question for the Speaker leaving the chair, unless its object be to prevent the sitting of the committee; as the amendment, if agreed to, supersedes the question for the Speaker leaving the Chair.[†]

Power to amend in committee limited.

No amendment which is irrelevant to the bill (as extending its operations beyond the limits expressed in the preamble and title, &c.) can be made without an instruction.[‡] If any amendment be made that is not within the title of the bill, the committee amend the title accordingly, and report the same specially to the House.[§]

Special instruction.

In the Session of 1852–3, the committee of the whole on the bill to empower the Municipal

* May, p. 461.
† May, p. 362.
‡ May, p. 474.
§ Standing Order, British House of Commons, 19th July, 1854. Bristowe, p. 133.

Council of the County of Two Mountains to sub-
scribe for stock in any railway passing through
that county, was instructed to inquire into the
expediency of the extending its provisions to the
County of Terrebonne. The bill was amended
accordingly and passed, and was subsequently
amended by the Legislative Council so as to extend its operation also to the counties of Rouville and Missisquoi.

When it may be found necessary to insert, in
a private bill, a clause affecting the public revenue,
property, or credit, the authority therefor must
(with the consent of the Government) emanate
from a committee of the whole; thus, in 1866,
the Canada Vine Growers' Association having
applied for an Act of incorporation, a bill was introduced and proceeded with in the ordinary way;
and the consent of the Government having been
obtained, a Resolution (originating in committee
of the whole) was passed by the House, exempt-
ing the wines made by the Association from
excise duties for a term of ten years; and the
Resolution was referred to the committee of the
whole on the bill, to make the necessary provision
therein. In 1867–8, this exemption was extended
for a further period of two years,—the same
course being taken as before.

When it is intended to propose any important
amendment in committee of the whole, or at the

Clauses affecting public revenue, &c., originate in committee of whole.

Notice to be given of amendments.

third reading, one day's notice thereof must be given.*

In the committee of the whole, the same course is adopted as in the select committee,—the question being proposed on the preamble first.† The chairman then reads the number of each clause in succession, with the marginal note which explains its objects. If no amendment be offered to a clause, he at once puts the question, " That this clause stand part of the bill," and proceeds to the next. When an amendment is proposed, he states the line in which the alteration is to be made, and puts the question in the ordinary form. No amendment can be made to a clause after the committee has passed on to another clause; nor can any amendment be offered to any clause which is irrelevant to the subject matter of such clause, but the same should be submitted, as a separate clause, at the end of the bill.‡ Clauses may be postponed, unless they have been amended, when it is not regular to postpone them. Postponed

Course of proceeding in committee of the whole.

Amendments.

Clauses postponed.

* 67th Rule. In the Commons of G. B., every such amendment is also, in all cases involving a necessity therefor, referred to the Committee on Standing Orders for their report. May, p. 728.

† In this respect differing from the course pursued upon public bills, the preamble of which is postponed until the clauses have been settled.

‡ May, p. 469.

clauses are considered after the other clauses are disposed of, and before any new clauses are brought up. If the committee cannot go through **Report.** the whole bill at one sitting, they direct the chairman to report progress, and ask leave to sit again. When the bill has been fully considered, the chairman puts a question, " That I do report this bill without amendment," or " with the amendments, to the House ;" which being agreed to, the sitting of the committee is concluded, and Mr Speaker resumes the chair : upon which the chairman approaches the steps of the Speaker's chair, and reports from the committee that " they had gone through the bill and had made amendments thereto," or that " they had gone through the bill and directed him to report the same without amendment." * Sometimes, however, the proceedings of a committee are brought to a close by an order " That the chairman do now leave the chair ;" in which case the chairman, being without instructions, makes no report to the House, and the bill disappears from the Order Book and is generally regarded as defunct ; but it is nevertheless competent for the House to appoint another day for the committee, and to proceed with the bill.†

---

* May, p. 476.
† May, p. 476.

**Proceed-
ings after
report.**

When the chairman has reported the bill to the House, the entire bill is open to consideration, and amendments may be made. and new clauses added (of which due notice has been given, as above mentioned), or the bill may be re-committed for further amendment.* If amendments have been made in committee, the question is at once put upon each amendment, in the order in which it stands in the bill ; or the consideration of the bill. as reported, may be postponed to a future day. If any of the amendments are supposed to be in excess of the Notice given by the promoters of the bill. the proper course is to refer them to the Committee on Standing Orders for their report.†

**Third read-
ing order-
ed.**

When the bill has been reported. and the amendments made in committee (if any) have been disposed of by the House, it is ordered for a third reading on the following day. The practice of engrossing on parchment, all bills ordered for a third reading, was discontinued in 1851, when both Houses agreed to substitute bills printed by the Queen's Printer, for the engrossed copies : a further change was made in 1862, when the printing of these bills was transferred to the Parliamentary contractors, with whom it still remains.

---

* May, p. 478.

† Ottawa & Prescott Railway, 1865 (Jan. Sess.): Cobourg & Peterboro' Railway, 1865 (Aug. Sess.)

13.—THIRD READING OF BILL.

Private bills on the Orders of the Day for a third reading, take precedence, on Private Bill days (see remarks under "Second reading of Bill" *supra*, p. 100) of all other Orders.* At this stage it is not customary to make any amendments but such as are merely verbal; no important amendment may be proposed without one day's notice thereof:† if it be considered necessary, the order for the third reading may be discharged, and the bill re-committed. Time for third reading.

This is usually the stage at which the Queen's consent is signified to any bill affecting the property or interests of the Crown.‡ Rights of the Crown.

The order for the third reading being read, the member in charge of the bill moves 1st, " That the bill be now read a third time; 2nd, " That the bill do now pass, and that the title be," &c. The Passage of bill.

Clerk is then ordered to carry the bill to the Senate, and desire their concurrence.

Every stage of a private bill, in its passage through the House of Commons, has now been described. It may be here mentioned, that, in accordance with the practice on public bills, a bill may, upon urgent and extraordinary occasions, be advanced two or more stages in one day,* but except in cases of urgent and pressing necessity, no motion may be made to dispense with any Standing Order relative to private bills without due notice,† printed in the Votes.

No Standing Order suspended without notice.

If a bill be subsequently returned from the Senate with amendments, the member in charge (or any other member acting for him) moves " That the amendments made by the Senate to the Bill (*title*) be now taken into consideration." They are then read by the Clerk a first time, and if merely verbal or unimportant, they are read a second time, and may be at once agreed to; the Clerk is then ordered to carry the bill to the Senate. If any of the amendments be important, they are referred to the Standing Committee to which the bill was originally referred,‡ and all further pro-

Bills amended by Senate.

Amendments referred, in certain cases.

---

* 43rd Rule.
† 69th Rule.
‡ 68th Rule. See Guelph & Lake Huron Railway, 1864; St. Charles Bridge, 1866; Port Hope, Lindsay & Beaverton Railway, 1866.

ceedings on the matter are suspended until their report is received.

The practice in the Senate with reference to any of their bills which may have been returned from the Commons with amendments, differs somewhat from that of the Commons in this respect,—leaving it optional to refer the amendments to the select committee, or to a committee of the whole.* Bills amended by Commons.

If the House disagree to one or more of the amendments, a committee is appointed to draw up the reasons for disagreeing, and they are communicated to the Senate at a conference,† and an opportunity is thus afforded to the Senate of not insisting upon the amendments objected to; or the reasons may be set forth in the motion for disagreeing, and communicated by message.‡ In the event of both Houses refusing to yield the point in discussion, the bill is withdrawn or abandoned.§ Amendments disagreed to.

In case a bill should not be proceeded with in the Senate, in consequence of amendments having been made which infringe the privileges of the Lower House, the same proceedings are adopted Bills not proceeded with in Senate.

---

* 60th Rule, Senate.
† Levis incorporation, 1861.
‡ Quebec Corporation, 1866.
§ Sherwood, p. 74.

as in case of a public bill. A committee is ap-

pointed to search the Journals of the Senate, and on their report, another bill may be ordered, including the amendments made by the Senate.*

---

* May, p. 733.

14.—PROCEEDINGS ON PRIVATE BILLS IN THE SENATE.

The proceedings on private bills in the Upper House differed materially from those in the Lower House, until the year 1861; but in that year the Legislative Council adopted Private Bill Rules identical with those of the Legislative Assembly. Some changes were made in these Rules by the House of Commons, in the first Session after Confederation,—the most important of which consisted in the reference of bills after the *first* instead of the *second* reading (hereinbefore referred to): this change, and certain minor alterations contingent upon it, were not adopted by the Senate, and bills before that House are therefore referred, as heretofore, after the second reading. In other respects the proceedings of the two Houses may be said to be identical.* When any such bill has been

Proceedings nearly identical with those of Commons.

Exception.

---

* The House of Lords have certain Standing Orders which are not common to both Houses. By one called the " Wharncliffe Order," it is provided that no bill empowering an existing company to execute or contribute to works, other than those for which it was originally constituted, or for the amalgamation,

Evidence. referred to a select or standing committee, the same course is taken for obtaining evidence upon the preamble; or the committee can, if they desire it, instruct their chairman to move that a message be sent to the Commons, requesting that the proofs and evidence on which the bill is founded may be communicated,* and these, when received, are referred to the committee.

Notice of sitting of committee. In the case of bills upon which notice by advertisement is required by the Rules, the committee give ~~twenty-four hours'~~ one peek's notice of their sitting.†

Origination of bills in either House. By far the greater number of private bills are introduced first in the Commons, but no arrangement has yet been effected between the two Houses, similar to that in operation in the Imperial Parliament, for regulating the class of bills which should originate in each House. A reference to

---

dissolution, or abandonment of the company, will be allowed to proceed without proof that a meeting of the proprietors was held, at which the bill was approved. There are also (under other of their Standing Orders) special matters required to be proved, or to be done, in certain classes of bills; and it is especially provided that no bill for the regulation of any trade, or the extension of the term of a patent, is to be read a second time, until a select committee has reported upon the expediency of taking it into further consideration. May, pp. 738 to 740.

* Pickering Harbour and Road Bill, 1852-3; Bill to remedy defects in title to Lot 4, Broken concession A and B. township of Hamilton, 1854-5.

† ~~44th~~ Rule, Senate.

the remarks on this subject in the Preliminary Chapter, and the corresponding Note, will explain the nature of this arrangement. (*supra*, p. 5.)

Divorce Bills are introduced first in the Senate, **Divorce Bills:** and there are certain Standing Orders concerning them which are peculiar to that House. On the presentation of the petition, a sum of $200 is deposited in the hands of the Clerk,* in place of **Fee.** the fee levied upon other private bills after the second reading. Notice of the application must be published in the Official-Gazette, and in two **Notice.** other newspapers, during six months before the presentation, instead of two months,† and various matters must be proved on the reading of the petition, which are specified in detail in the Chapter headed "Proof of Notices," &c. (*supra*, p. 38.) The bill, when presented, cannot be read a **First and** second time until 14 days shall have elapsed from **second reading of** the first reading: a notice of the day appointed **bill.** therefor, with a copy of the bill, are served on the party from whom the divorce is sought; and proof, on oath, of such service (where the same is possible) is adduced at the Bar before the second reading.‡ The petitioner attends below the **Attend-** Bar, at the second reading, to be examined gene- **ance of petitioner.** rally, or as to any collusion between the parties

---

* 83rd ~~64th~~ Rule, Senate.

† 72nd Rule, Senate.

‡ 77th Rule, Senate.

7*

to obtain a separation, unless such attendance is dispensed with.[*]   After the second reading, witnesses are examined ~~at the Bar~~, on oath, in support of the bill, the preliminary evidence being that (by certificate or otherwise) of the due celebration of the marriage of the parties.[†]   The counsel for each party may be heard at the Bar, either on the evidence, or on the provision for the future support of the wife.[‡]   Witnesses are notified by a summons under the hand and seal of the Speaker, served at the expense of the party applying therefor, by whom also their expenses are defrayed.[§]   Any witness refusing to attend is taken into the custody of the Usher of the Black Rod, and is liable for all expenses attending such default.[||]   After the second reading, the bill is referred, not to a select or standing committee, but to a committee of the whole House.[¶]   No bill to dissolve a marriage on the ground of adultery is received, without a clause prohibiting the offending party from marrying; but this clause is struck out in committee, or on the report, except in very peculiar cases.[**]   In all subsequent

Marginal notes:
Examination of witnesses. *a select committee of members, the evidence is taken down in preparation to the* **Counsel.**

Summons for witnesses.

Bill referred to committee of whole.

Prohibitory clause.

---

[*] 27th Rule, Senate.
[†] 78th Rule, Senate.
[‡] 80th Rule, Senate.
[§] 80th Rule, Senate.
[||] 82nd Rule, Senate.
[¶] May, p. 757.
[**] May (Edit. of 1855), p. 611.

proceedings, divorce bills are dealt with in the same manner as other private bills. If any matter not provided for by the Rules should arise, reference is had to the Rules and practice of the House of Lords.* When the bill is reported, and any amendments that may have been made are disposed of by the House, it is ordered to be read a third time on a future day, when it is read a third time, passed, and sent to the Commons in the usual form. Unprovided cases.

Bills for the reversal of attainders, or for the restoration of honors and lands, are first signed by the Governor General, and are presented in the Senate (without a previous petition) by command of His Excellency;† after which they pass through the ordinary stages, and are sent to the Commons. Here the Queen's consent is signified before the first reading; and if this form be overlooked, the proceedings will be null and void. After the second reading,‡ they may be ordered to be read a third time on a subsequent day, without reference to a committee. Such bills receive Reversal of attainders, &c.

---

* 64th Rule, Senate.

† Matthews' attainder reversal; Council Journ., 1846, p. 147.

‡ In the British House of Commons, such bills, after the second reading, are committed to several members specially nominated, "and all the members of this House who are of Her Majesty's most honorable Privy Council, and all the gentlemen of the long robe." May, p. 750.

the Royal Assent in the usual form, as public bills.*

The bills sent down to the Commons pass through the same stages, and are subject to the same rules, as other private bills, except that divorce bills are referred to a selected instead of a standing committee. When any private bill (not being a divorce bill)† is so received, that is not based on a petition which has been already reported on by the Committee on Standing Orders, it is taken into consideration and reported on by the said committee, after the first reading,‡ with reference to the notices required by the Rules.

* May, p. 751.
† May, p. 757.
‡ 54th Rule.

15.—ROYAL ASSENT.

Private bills receive the Royal Assent in the same manner and form, and at the same time, as public bills. Heretofore, every private Act, almost without exception, contained a clause declaring that it "shall be deemed a public Act." The effect of this clause was that it should be construed as an enactment that such Act should be judicially noticed by all Judges, Justices of the Peace and others, without being specially pleaded; whereas private Acts which did not contain such a clause could be judicially noticed only when specially pleaded. But by the "Interpretation Act" passed in 1867, it is expressly provided that "every Act shall, unless by express provision it is declared to be a Private Act, be deemed to be a Public Act, and shall be judicially noticed by all Judges, Justices of the Peace, and others, without being specially pleaded ; and all copies of Acts printed by the Queen's Printer, shall be evidence of such Acts and of their contents." *

"Public Act" clause.

All Acts now deemed to be Public Acts.

---

* 31 Vic., cap. 1, sec. 7., sub-sec. 35.

Until the year 1849, private Acts were printed *Printing of private acts with the Statutes.* with the public statutes, and bound together in the same volume. In that year, an Act was passed* which provided that local Acts should be printed (at the expense of the Province) in such number only as should suffice for distribution to the Judges, Public Departments, and certain local functionaries; and that of private or personal Acts, 150 copies only should be printed, at the expense of the parties obtaining the same. Under this arrangement no private Acts of any class were printed for general distribution with the Statutes; and the inconvenience attending it was so strongly felt, that in 1851 an Act was passed† providing for the printing and distribution of all local, private, and personal Acts, in the same manner, and to the same extent as the public Acts,—reviving, in fact, the former practice of binding up all the Acts of a Session, public and private, in the same volume. But by the "Interpretation Act" of 1867, it is provided that the Governor in Council may direct the distribution of the Statutes in such manner, either by the binding of the Public General Acts, and Acts of a local or private character, in separate volumes, or by binding them together in the same volumes

---

* 12 Vic. cap. 16.

† 14, 15 Vic., cap. 81.

with separate indexes or otherwise, as may be deemed expedient.*　　It may be worthy of consideration whether the public convenience would not be sufficiently consulted by printing a limited number (say 500 copies) of the local and private Acts, binding them in a supplementary volume, and distributing them with the public Acts only where they are really required.† This would cause a large saving in the cost of printing, and would disencumber the Statute Book of a mass of enactments which have no bearing on the statute law of the land.

---

* 31 Vic., cap. 1, sec. 13.

† All such private Acts of the Imperial Parliament as contain the "public" clause are printed in a separate collection, and are known as local or personal Acts. Another class, consisting chiefly of inclosure, drainage, and estate Acts, are printed by the Queen's Printers, and contain a clause declaring that a copy so printed "shall be admitted as evidence thereof by all judges, justices and others," and a further enactment that the "Act shall not be deemed a public Act." A third class, consisting of name, naturalization, divorce, and other strictly personal Acts, are not printed; but a list of them is inserted by the Queen's Printers after the titles of the other private Acts. May, pp. 759, 760.

11

APPENDIX I.

RULES COMMON TO BOTH HOUSES

IN RELATION TO

PRIVATE BILLS.

Petitions for Private Bills. 49. No Petition for any Private Bill is received by The House [Senate] after the first ~~three weeks~~ /10 days/ of each Session ; nor may any Private Bill be presented to The House [Senate] after the first ~~four~~ weeks of each Session ; nor may any Report of any Standing or Select Committee upon a Private Bill be received after the first six weeks of each Session. [And no Motion for the general suspension or modification of this Rule shall be entertained by The House, unless after reference made thereof at a previous sitting of The House, to the ~~several Standing~~ Committees ~~charged with consideration of Private Bills~~, or upon Report submitted by two or more ~~of such~~ Committees.]*

This sentence occurs in the Commons Rule only.

50. The Clerk of The House [Senate] shall, during each Recess of Parliament, publish weekly in the Official "Canada" Gazette, the following Rules respecting Notices of intended applications for Private Bills, and ~~in other newspapers (English and French)~~ the substance thereof; ~~and shall also, im~~mediately after the issue of the Proclamation convening Parliament for the despatch of business, publish in the Official Gazette, and in other newspapers, as aforesaid, until the opening of Parliament, the day on which the time limited for receiving Petitions for Private Bills will ex~~pire, pursuant to the foregoing Rule~~ ; and the Clerk shall also announce, by notice affixed in the committee rooms and lobbies of this House [the Senate] by the first day of every Session, the time limited for receiving Petitions for Private Bills, and Private Bills, and Reports thereon.

Publication by the Clerk, of Rules relative to Notice, &c.

51. All applications for Private Bills, properly the subjects of legislation by the Parliament of Canada within the purview of " The British North America Act, 1867," whether for the erection of a Bridge, the making of a Railroad, Turnpike Road, or Telegraph Line ; the construction or improvement of a Harbour, Canal, Lock, Dam or Slide, or other like work; the granting of a right of Ferry ; the incorporation of any particular Trade or Calling, or of any Banking or other Joint Stock Company ; or otherwise for granting to any

Notices for Private Bills.

individual or individuals any exclusive or peculiar rights or privileges whatever, or for doing any
matter or thing which in its operation would
affect the rights or property of other parties, or
relate to any particular class of the community;
or for making any amendment of a like nature to
any former Act,—shall require a Notice, clearly
*e ys·per... fxc·····*and distinctly specifying the nature and object
dsp confuration)of the application, to be published as follows,
d in relief q th)viz.:— *and Manitoba*

*In the Provinces of Quebec—*A Notice inserted in
Notices for Private Bills. the Official Gazette, in the English and French
languages, and in one newspaper in the English,
and one newspaper in the French language, in
the District affected, or in both languages if
there be but one paper; or if there be no paper
published therein, then (in both languages) in
the Official Gazette, and in a paper published in
an adjoining District.

*In any other Province—*A Notice inserted in the
Official Gazette, and in one newspaper published
in the County, or Union of Counties, affected, or
if there be no paper published therein, then in a
newspaper in the next nearest County in which
a newspaper is published.

Such Notices shall be continued in each case
for a period of at least two months, during the interval of time between the close of the next pre-

ceding Session and the consideration of the Petition.

52. Before any Petition praying for leave to Toll Bridge
bring in a Private Bill for the erection of a Toll-
bridge, is presented to the House [Senate], the
person or persons intending to petition for such
Bill, shall, upon giving the Notice prescribed
by the preceding Rule, also, at the same time, and
in the same manner, give Notice of the Rates
which they intend to ask, the extent of the
privilege, the height of the arches, the interval
between the abutments or piers for the passage of
rafts and vessels, and mentioning also whether
they intend to erect a drawbridge or not, and
the dimensions of the same.

53. Petitions for Private Bills, when received Petitions
by The House [Senate], are to be taken into con- to be reported on
sideration (without special reference) by the Com- by Standing Orders
mittee on Standing Orders; which is to report in Committee
each case, whether the Rules with regard to Notice have been complied with; and in every case
where the Notice shall prove to have been insufficient, either as regards the Petition as a whole, or
any matter therein which ought to have been
specially referred to in the Notice, the Committee
is to recommend to The House [Senate] the course
to be taken in consequence of such insufficiency
of Notice.

54. All Private Bills from the Senate [House of

Private
Bills from
Senate.

Commons], (not being based on a Petition which
has already been so reported on by the Committee)
shall be first taken into consideration and reported on by the said Committee in like manner, after
the First Reading of such Bills, and before their
consideration by any other Standing Committee.

55. No Motion for the suspension of the Rules
upon any Petition for a Private Bill is entertained,
unless the same has been reported upon by the
Committee on Standing Orders.

Suspension
of Rules.

56. All Private Bills are introduced on Petition,
and presented to The House [Senate], [upon a
motion for leave, ~~to be made on a Monday, Wednesday, or Friday, immediately before the calling
of the Orders for Private Bills. and *~~] after such
Petition has been favorably reported on by the
Committee on Standing Orders.

Introduc-
tion of
Private
Bills.

57. When any Bill for confirming any Letters
Patent or Agreement is presented to The House,
[Senate] a true copy of such Letters Patent or
Agreement must be attached to it.

Letters
Patent, or
Agree-
ments.

~~58. The expense and cost attending on Private~~
Bills giving any exclusive privilege, or for any
object of profit, or private or corporate or individual advantage, or for amending, extending,
or enlarging any former Acts, in such manner as
~~to confer additional powers, ought not to fall on~~

Fees, and
cost of pre-
paring and
printing
Private
Bills.

~~the public; accordingly the parties seeking to~~ Fees and
obtain any such Bill, shall be required to pay into charges.
the Private Bill Office the sum of one hundred
dollars, immediately after the [First Reading *]
thereof: and all such bills shall be prepared in the
English and French languages, by the parties applying for the same, and printed by the Contractor for printing the Bills of The House [Senate],
and 500 copies thereof in English and 200 copies
in French shall be deposited in the Private Bill
Office [and distribution thereof made, before the
First Reading †]; and no such Bill shall be read
a Third time until a certificate from the Queen's
Printer shall have been fyled with The Clerk,
that the cost of printing 500 copies of the Act in
English and 250 in French, for the Government,
has been paid to him.

The Fee payable on the [First Reading *] of Fee, and
any Private Bill is paid only in the House in which cost of
printing,
such Bill originates, but the cost of printing the where paid.
same is paid in each House.

59. Every Private Bill, when read a [First time Bills and
‡] is referred to the Committee on Private Bills, Petitions
referred.
if any such shall have been appointed, or to some
~~other Standing Committee of the same character~~;

---

* "*Second* reading," in Senate Rule.

† In the Senate Rule, the words "before second reading,"
occur in place of those between brackets.

‡ "*Second* time," in Senate Rule.

~~and all Petitions before The House [Senate] for or against the Bill are considered as referred to such Committee.~~

COMMONS. | SENATE.

Sitting of Committee

60. No Committee on any Private Bill, originating in this House, of which Notice is required to be given, is to consider the same until after ~~(one week)~~ ~~ten clear days'~~ Notice of the Sitting of such Committee has been first affixed in the Lobby; nor, in the case of any such Bill originating in the Senate, until after ~~two~~ ~~24 hours~~ ~~days'~~ like Notice. And no Motion for any general suspension or modification of this Rule, shall be entertained by the House, unless after reference made thereof at a previous sitting of The House, to the several Standing Committees charged with consideration of Private Bills, or upon Report submitted by two or more of such Committees.

2. On the day of the posting of any Bill under this Rule, the ~~Chief~~ Clerk of the ~~Private Bill Office~~, shall append to the printed Votes and Proceedings of the day, a Notice of such posting: ~~and he shall~~ also append to the Votes of each day, a Notice of the meetings of any of the Standing Committees charged with the consideration of Private Bills or Petitions therefor, that may have been appointed for ~~the following day.~~

61. No Committee on any Private Bill originating in the Senate, of which Notice is required to be given, is to consider the same until after a week's notice of the Sitting of such Committee, has been first affixed in the Lobby; nor, in the case of any such Bill originating in the House of Commons, until after twenty-four hours' like notice.

Senate only [54. A copy of the Bill containing the Amendments proposed to be submitted to the Standing Committee, shall be deposited in the Private Bill Office, one clear day before the meeting of the Committee thereupon.] Deposit of filled up Bill in Private Bill Office.

61 62. All persons whose interest or property may be affected by any Private Bill, shall, when required so to do, appear before the Standing Committee touching their consent, or may send such consent in writing, proof of which may be demanded by such Committee. And in every case, the Committee upon any Bill for incorporating a Company, may require proof that the persons whose names appear in the Bill as composing the Company, are of full age, and in a position to effect the objects contemplated, and have consented to become incorporated. Consent of parties interested.

62 63. All questions before Committees on Private Bills are decided by a majority of voices, including the voice of the Chairman; and whenever the voices are equal, the Chairman has a second or casting vote. Voting in committees

63 64. It is the duty of the Select Committee to which any Private Bill may be referred by The House [Senate], to call the attention of The House [Senate] specially to any provision inserted in such Bill that does not appear to have been contemplated in the Notice for the same, as reported upon by the Committee on Standing Orders. Extraordinary provisions in Bills.

64 65. The Committee to which a Private Bill

Report of Committee. may have been referred, shall report the same to The House [Senate], in every case; and when any material alteration has been made in the Preamble of the Bill, such alteration, and the reasons for the same, are to be stated in the Report.

Preamble not proved. 65 N. When the Committee on any Private Bill report to The House [Senate] that the Preamble of such Bill has not been proved to their satisfaction, they must also state the grounds upon which they have arrived at such a decision; and no Bill so reported upon shall be placed upon the Orders of the Day unless by special order of The House [Senate].

[2. Private Bills otherwise reported to The House by such Committee, shall be placed upon the Orders of the Day following the reception of the Report, for ~~a second reading~~, in the proper order, next after Bills referred to a Committee of the Whole House.*]

Chairman to sign Bills and Amendments. 66 N. The Chairman of the Committee shall sign with his name at length, a printed copy of the Bill, on which the Amendments are fairly written, and shall also sign with the initials of his name, the several Amendments made and Clauses added in Committee; and another copy of the Bill, with the amendments written thereon, shall be prepared by the Clerk of the Committee, and fyled

---

This paragraph occurs in the Commons Rule only.

in the Private Bill Office. or attached to the Report.

67 66. No important Amendment may be proposed to any Private Bill, in a Committee of the Whole House. or at the Third Reading of the Bill, unless one day's notice of the same shall have been given.

Amendments by the House.

68. When any Private Bill is returned from the Senate [House of Commons] with amendments, the same not being merely verbal or unimportant, such amendments are, previous to the Second Reading, referred to [a Committee of the Whole, or to *] the Standing Committee to which such Bill was originally referred.

Bill amended by Senate.

69 70. Except in cases of urgent and pressing necessity, no Motion may be made to dispense with any Standing Order relative to Private Bills, without due notice thereof.

Dispensing with Standing Orders.

70. A Book, to be called the "Private Bill Register," shall be kept ~~in a room to be called the "Private Bill Office,"~~ in which Book shall be entered, by the Clerk appointed for that business ~~of that Office,~~ the name, description. and place of residence of the parties applying for the Bill, or of their agent, and all the proceedings thereon, from the Petition to the passing of the Bill; such entry to specify briefly each proceeding in The House [Senate], or in any Committee to which

Private Bill Register.

---

* These words occur in the Senate Rule only.

the Bill or Petition may be referred, and the day on which the Committee is appointed to sit. Such book to be open to public inspection daily, during Office hours.

Private Bill Committees.

718. The [Chief] Clerk of the [Private Bill Office] shall [prepare, daily], lists of all Private Bills, and Petitions for such Bills, upon which any Committee is appointed to sit, specifying the time of meeting and the room where the Committee shall sit; and the same shall be hung up in the Lobby.

(The following Rules may also be given, as bearing on the practice in Parliament in relation to Private as well as Public Bills.)

(Senate.)

Unprovided cases, Senate.

112—In all unprovided cases, the rules, usages, and forms of the House of Lords are to be followed.

(Commons.)

Parliamentary Agents.

72—Every Parliamentary Agent conducting proceedings before the House of Commons, shall be personally responsible to the House and to the Speaker for the observance of the rules, orders and practice of Parliament, and rules prescribed by the Speaker, and also for the payment of all fees and charges; and he shall not act as a

---

* In Commons Rule only.

Parliamentary Agent until he shall have received
the express sanction and authority of the Speaker.

73<del>74</del>.—Any Agent who shall wilfully act in vio- Agents
lation of the rules and practice of Parliament, or Rules lia-
of any rules to be prescribed by the Speaker, or pension.
who shall wilfully misconduct himself in prose-
cuting any proceedings before Parliament, shall
be liable to an absolute or temporary prohibition
to practise as a Parliamentary Agent, at the
pleasure of the Speaker ; provided that upon the
application of such Agent, the Speaker shall state
in writing the ground for such prohibition.

§7 <del>116</del>.—In all unprovided cases, the rules, usages Unprovid-
and forms of the House of Commons of the United Commons.
Kingdom of Great Britain and Ireland shall be
followed.

12

APPENDIX II.

RULES OF THE SENATE

CONCERNING

BILLS OF DIVORCE.

Divorce notices published.

72. Every Applicant for a Bill of Divorce is required to give Notice of his intended application, and to specify from whom and for what cause, by advertisement during six months, in the *Official Gazette*, and in two newspapers published in the District, in Quebec and manitoba, or County or Union of Counties in the other provinces, where such Applicant usually resided at the time of the separation, or if the requisite number of papers cannot be found therein, then in the adjoining District, or County or union of Counties manitoba.

The Notice for the Provinces of Quebec, is to be published in the English and French languages.

And served on ad-

73N. A copy of the Notice, in writing, is to be served, at the instance of the Applicant, upon

the person from whom the Divorce is sought, if **verse party.**
the residence of such person can be ascertained;
and proof on Oath of such service, or of the
attempts made to effect it to the satisfaction of
The Senate, is to be adduced before The Senate
on the reading of the Petition.

74 N. When Proceedings in any Courts of Law **Proceedings in Courts filed.** have taken place prior to the Petition, an exemplification of such Proceedings to final judgment, duly certified, is to be presented to The Senate, on the reading of the Petition.

75 N. In cases where damages have been award-**Damages levied.** ed to the Applicant, proof on Oath must be adduced, to the satisfaction of The Senate, that such damages have been levied and retained, or explanation given to The Senate for the neglect or inability to levy the same under a writ of execution, as they may deem a sufficient excuse for such omission.

76 N. The Second Reading of the Bill is not to **Formalities before 2nd reading.** take place until fourteen days after the first reading, and Notice of such second reading is to be affixed upon the Doors of The Senate during that period, and a copy thereof, and of the Bill, duly served upon the party from whom the Divorce is sought; and proof, on Oath, of such Service, adduced at the Bar of The Senate, before proceeding to the second reading, or sufficient

proof adduced of the impossibility of complying
with this regulation.

77N. The petitioner is to appear below the Bar

Petitioner
to appear.

of The Senate, at the second reading, to ~~be~~
examined by the Senate, generally, or as to any
collusion or connivance between the parties to
obtain such separation, unless The Senate think
fit to dispense therewith.

is referred to the
committee 79
no —

78 N. After the Second Reading, Witnesses are to

Evidence
of celebra-
tion of
marriage.

~~be~~ heard ~~at the Bar of The Senate~~ on Oath; the
preliminary evidence being that of the due cele-
bration of the marriage between the parties, by
legitimate testimony, either by witnesses present
at the time of the marriage, or by complete and
satisfactory proof of the certificate of the officiat-
ing minister or authority.

79N. The Counsel for the Applicant, as well as

Counsel
heard.

the party from whom the Divorce is sought, may
be heard before the Bar of The Senate, as well on
the evidence adduced, as on the provisions for the
future support of the wife, if deemed necessary.

80. The Witnesses are notified to attend by a

Witnesses,
how sum-
moned.

Summons, to issue under the hand and seal of
The Speaker, to the parties applying for the same,
on application to The Clerk of The Senate, and
served at the expense of the said parties, by the
Usher of the Black Rod, or his authorized Deputy;
and every Witness is allowed his reasonable

(which, with those incurred by the taking of the Black Rod or his deputy were)
~~expenses,~~ to be taxed by The Senate, or any
Officer thereof appointed for that purpose.

81 82. Witnesses refusing to obey the Summons *When re-fusing to attend.*
are, by Order of the Senate, taken into the custody
of the Usher of the Black Rod, and not liberated
therefrom, except by Order of The Senate, and
after payment of the expenses incurred.

82. Every Bill of Divorce is to be prepared in *Bill pre-pared and printed by petitioner.*
the English and French languages by the party
applying for the same, and printed by the Contractor for the Sessional Printing for The Senate,
at the expense of the party; and ~~five~~ *six* hundred
copies thereof, in English, and two hundred
copies in French, must be deposited in the Office
of The Clerk of The Senate, and no such Bill is
to be read a third time until a certificate from the
Queen's Printer shall have been filed with The
Clerk, that the cost of printing 500 copies of the
Act in English, and 250 copies in French for the
Government, has been paid to him.

23 84. Every applicant for a Bill of Divorce, at *Amount to be paid.*
the time of presenting the Petition, is to pay into
the hands of The Clerk of The Senate, a sum of
Two ~~One~~ hundred dollars, to cover the expenses
which may be incurred by the Senate during the
progress of the Bill.

84 85. In all unprovided cases, reference should *Unprovid-ed cases.*
be had to the Rules and Decisions of the House
of Lords.

APPENDIX III.

FORM OF PETITION TO THE THREE BRANCHES OF THE
LEGISLATURE, FOR A PRIVATE BILL.

Form of
Petition to
His Excel-
lency.

To His Excellency the Right Honorable Sir
John Young, Baronet, K.C.B., G.C.M.G.,
Governor General of Canada, &c., &c., &c.,

IN COUNCIL.

The Petition of the undersigned   of the
of

HUMBLY SHEWETH:

That (*here state the object de-
sired by the petitioner in soliciting an Act*).

Wherefore your petitioner humbly prays that
Your Excellency may be pleased to sanction
the passing of an Act (*for the purposes above
mentioned*).

And as in duty bound, your petitioner will ever
pray.

(Signature) { Seal, in the case
of an existing
Corporation.

(*Date.*)

(*To either House.*)

To the Honorable the { Senate
{ House of Commons }
of Canada, in Parliament assembled :

The Petition of the undersigned   of the
            of

HUMBLY SHEWETH :

            That (*here state the object de-
sired by the petitioner in soliciting an Act.*)

    Wherefore your petitioner humbly prays that
        Your Honorable House may be pleased
        to pass an Act (*for the purposes above men-
        tioned*).

    And as in duty bound, your petitioner will
        ever pray.

                    (Signature)   { Seal, as above.

(*Date.*)

INDEX.

———

13

INDEX.

*Private Bills—*continued.

Proceedings in House, after report of committee of whole, 108.

Re-commitment of bill, to standing committee, 95 ;—to committee of the whole, 108.

Third reading, 109.

Queen's consent signified at this stage, when rights of Crown are affected, 109.

Bill passed and sent to Senate, 109.

Returned from the Senate, with amendments ; amendments referred, 110.

Conference desired on disagreeing to certain amendments, 111.

Bills from the Commons not proceeded with in the Senate; committee appointed to search journals, 111.

Proceedings on private bills in Senate, 113.

Royal Assent, 119.

Every Act declared " public" that does not contain a provision declaring it " private," 119.

Printing of Private Acts, 120.

Arrangement (in certain Sessions) for taking up at the next Session, any private bills undisposed of at the prorogation, 62.

Private Bill Committee (or other committees of a like character) :

Appointment and powers, 64.

All private bills referred to this (or some similar) committee; Petitions for and against stand referred, 56, 127.

Committee may be directed to report a bill back forthwith, 65.

Instructions, 65.—Solicited by committee with regard to a doubtful point, 93 ;—an extension of their powers in a certain case, 66.

To call attention to any provisions in the bill not covered by the notice, 66.

To require proof of the qualification and consent of persons proposed to be incorporated, 67.

Not to entertain questions relative to compliance with standing orders (notices) unless specially directed, 67.

To give notice of day appointed for consideration of certain bills, 71, 128.

Te ascertain whether the provisions of the bill agree with the terms of the notice, 68.

Casting vote of chairman, 69, 129.

Each member of committee present should vote on every question, 69.

Committee cannot sit (without special leave) during sitting of the House, 70.

—Leave given, in Imperial Parliament, to sit during morning sittings of House, 70. (Note.)

ndex entries:

INDEX.

Savings Banks :
Placed under control of the Parliament of Canada, 13.

Second reading of bill :
Principle affirmed at the second reading, 97.
Postponement thereof 3 or 6 months, 100.
Opposition at this stage unusual, 98.
Counsel heard at second reading, 98.
Referred after second reading (in *Senate,* to a standing committee), 57 ; 127
~~(in Commons, to a committee of whole), 101.~~
A bill thrown out in the Commons (G. B.) at this stage, because it trenched on public rights, 99. (Note.)

Semi-private bills :
Certain bills of this class treated as public bills, 7.

Senate :
Assimilation of their Private Bill Rules to those of the Commons, 3.— Exceptions, 113.
Bills from the Senate reported on by Committee on Standing Orders after first reading, when no previous report has been made on a petition, 35, 125.
Divorce Bills introduced first in the Senate, 5.—Bills for reversal of attainders, or for the restoration of honors, 117.
Proof of notice, and other preliminary proceedings in Divorce cases, in the Senate, 39.
Bills presented in the Senate, without a motion for leave, 54. (Note.)
Evidence taken on bills originating in the Senate, communicated to committee of the Commons, when required, 87.—The like, in the Senate, with regard to bills originating in the Commons, 114.
Amendments of the Senate to bills from the Commons, are referred to the same committee of the Commons to which the bill was originally referred, 110, 131.—Practice in Senate with regard to amendments of the Commons, 111, 131.
Conference with the Senate on disagreeing to their amendments to bills, 111.
Journals of Senate may be searched by a Committee of Commons, with reference to certain bills not proceeded with, 111.
Proceedings on private bills in the Senate, 113.

14

FINIS.

www.ingramcontent.com/pod-product-compliance
Lightning Source LLC
Chambersburg PA
CBHW020545270326
41927CB00006B/729